The Ultimate Nicoise Salad Cookbook: 101 Delicious Recipes for Every Occasion

Cafe Mocha

Contents

INTRODUCTION 7

1. Apple-Cinnamon SlingTraditional Nicoise Salad 8

2. Mediterranean Nicoise Salad..8

3. Avocado Nicoise Salad 9

4. Grilled Vegetable Nicoise Salad 10

5. Roasted Butternut Squash Nicoise Salad 11

6. Cucumber Nicoise Salad 12

7. Nicoise Salad with Fried Egg..13

8. Nicoise Salad with Tuna..14

9. Nicoise Salad with Shrimp 15

10. Nicoise Salad with Olives..16

11. Nicoise Salad with Baby Potatoes..17

12. Nicoise Salad with Artichoke Hearts..18

13. Nicoise Salad with Roasted Red Peppers 18

14. Nicoise Salad with Feta Cheese...19

15. Nicoise Salad with Sun-Dried Tomatoes..20

16. Nicoise Salad with Prosciutto..21

17. Nicoise Salad with Capers..22

18. Nicoise Salad with Sweet Potatoes 23

19. Nicoise Salad with Warm Bacon..24

20. Nicoise Salad with Anchovies 25

21. Nicoise Salad with Avocado and Grapefruit.....................................26

22. Nicoise Salad with Mozzarella...27

23. Nicoise Salad with Quinoa...28

24. Nicoise Salad with Edamame 28

25. Nicoise Salad with Beets 29

26. Nicoise Salad with Scallops...30

27. Nicoise Salad with Asparagus..31

28. Nicoise Salad with Poached Egg......................32

29. Nicoise Salad with Radishes 33

30. Nicoise Salad with Arugula.............................34

31. Nicoise Salad with Chickpeas.........................35

32. Nicoise Salad with Green Beans 36

33. Nicoise Salad with Goat Cheese 37

34. Nicoise Salad with Roasted Garlic.................38

35. Nicoise Salad with Seared Tuna.....................39

36. Nicoise Salad with Lemon Basil Vinaigrette ...40

37. Nicoise Salad with Avocado and Bacon.........41

38. Nicoise Salad with Dried Cranberries 42

39. Nicoise Salad with Artichoke Hearts and Olives 43

40. Nicoise Salad with Fennel and Dill................43

41. Nicoise Salad with Pomegranate Seeds..........44

42. Nicoise Salad with Orzo................................45

43. Nicoise Salad with Crispy Shallots.................46

44. Nicoise Salad with Radicchio 48

45. Nicoise Salad with Paprika Roasted Potatoes.........48

46. Nicoise Salad with Chive Vinaigrette.............50

47. Nicoise Salad with Marinated Mushrooms.......51

48. Nicoise Salad with Roasted Asparagus 52

49. Nicoise Salad with Toasted Almonds 53

50. Nicoise Salad with Red Onions......................54

51. Nicoise Salad with Balsamic Mustard Dressing.........55

52. Nicoise Salad with Roasted Red Bell Peppers 56

53. Nicoise Salad with Fresh Basil 57

54. Nicoise Salad with Anchovy Vinaigrette 58

55. Nicoise Salad with Oven Roasted Tomatoes.........59

56. Nicoise Salad with Cherry Tomatoes 60

57. Nicoise Salad with Fregola 61

58. Nicoise Salad with Farro 62

59. Nicoise Salad with Radish Sprouts 63

60. Nicoise Salad with Sesame Seeds 63

61. Nicoise Salad with Wasabi Peas 64

62. Nicoise Salad with Sauteed Prawns 65

63. Nicoise Salad with Pickled Onions 67

64. Nicoise Salad with Mango 68

65. Nicoise Salad with Roasted Parsnips 69

66. Nicoise Salad with Black Olives 70

67. Nicoise Salad with Macadamia Nuts 70

68. Nicoise Salad with Soft Boiled Egg 71

69. Nicoise Salad with Camembert Cheese 72

70. Nicoise Salad with Mustard Vinaigrette 73

71. Nicoise Salad with White Beans 74

72. Nicoise Salad with Grilled Halloumi 75

73. Nicoise Salad with Spring Onion 76

74. Nicoise Salad with Paprika Tuna 77

75. Nicoise Salad with Pickled Red Cabbage 78

76. Nicoise Salad with Edamame Hummus 79

77. Nicoise Salad with Curried Chickpeas 80

78. Nicoise Salad with Saffron Aioli 81

79. Nicoise Salad with Avocado and Figs 82

80. Nicoise Salad with Pickled Fennel 83

81. Nicoise Salad with Roasted Butternut Squash and Hazelnuts 84

82. Nicoise Salad with Cucumber Ribbon Salad 85

83. Nicoise Salad with Roasted Brussels Sprouts 86

84. Nicoise Salad with Creamy Horseradish Dressing 87

85. Nicoise Salad with Seared Tuna Steak 88

86. Nicoise Salad with Red Quinoa..89

87. Nicoise Salad with Fried Capers 90

88. Nicoise Salad with Pickled Mustard Seed Dressing.........................91

89. Nicoise Salad with Toasted Sesame Seeds..................................92

90. Nicoise Salad with Smoked Salmon 93

91. Nicoise Salad with Roasted Walnuts 94

92. Nicoise Salad with Pickled Asparagus......................................95

93. Nicoise Salad with Caviar...96

94. Nicoise Salad with Grilled Eggplant..97

95. Nicoise Salad with Crispy Shallots and Chives..............................98

96. Nicoise Salad with Roasted Carrots..99

97. Nicoise Salad with Red Wine Vinaigrette.................................100

98. Nicoise Salad with Honey Mustard Dressing 101

99. Nicoise Salad with Orange Slices...102

100. Nicoise Salad with Radishes and Asparagus..............................103

101. Nicoise Salad with Roasted Prosciutto and Pine 104

CONCLUSION 106

INTRODUCTION

Welcome to The Ultimate Nicoise Salad Cookbook: 101 Delicious Recipes for Every Occasion! This cookbook combines traditional French flavors with the healthiest and freshest ingredients for a delicious twist on the classic Nicoise salad. With our collection of recipes, you can create tantalizing salads for every occasion.

The Nicoise salad is a favorite staple in France and has become increasingly popular in other places around the world. This classic salad is traditionally composed of tuna, boiled eggs, potatoes, tomatoes, black olives, anchovies, and vinaigrette. This one-dish meal has been prepared the same way since the end of the 19th century and is known for its colorful presentation and traditional flavors.

In The Ultimate Nicoise Salad Cookbook: 101 Delicious Recipes for Every Occasion, you will find a comprehensive and inspiring collection of recipes for Nicoise salads. All our recipes are easy to prepare and use the freshest and healthiest ingredients so you get the most out of your salad. We have included recipes for all occasions, from light and refreshing meals for summer and spring, to healthy and hearty salads for winter.

In the Summer section, you'll find recipes such as our Mediterranean Nicoise Salad, a colorful array of vegetables, tuna and feta in a vinaigrette dressing, and Grilled Shrimp Nicoise Salad, with succulent grilled shrimp and the richest ingredients. If you're looking for something a bit more hearty, you can try our Winter Vegetable Nicoise Salad, a savory blend of root vegetables, crumbled cheese, and a honey mustard dressing.

For lighter meals, our Spring Nicoise Salads are a great option, including recipes like Seared Tuna Poke Nicoise Salad and Spicy Tuna Nicoise Salad, both with delicious Asian-inspired flavors. The Spring section also includes recipes for Fruit Salads, like our Mango and Tomato Nicoise Salad and Apple and Avocado Nicoise Salad.

With our 101 Nicoise salads, there is something for every occasion, from simple, bright salads for lunch, to hearty winter dishes for dinner. We hope our cookbook inspires you to create delicious and nutritious dishes that will please your family and friends - bon appétit!

1. Apple-Cinnamon SlingTraditional Nicoise Salad

Apple-Cinnamon Sling is a refreshingly delicious twist on a classic cocktail. This cocktail combines the sweetness of apples and cinnamon with a bit of caramel to deliver a delightful flavor that is sure to tantalize your taste buds.

Serves: 4; | Preparation Time: 10 minutes; | Ready Time: 10 minutes;

Ingredients:
- 2 tablespoons applesauce,
- 1 shot of caramel syrup,
- 1 tablespoon of ground cinnamon,
- 1 shot of vodka, 2 tablespoons of lime juice,
- 2 tablespoons of orange juice;

Instructions:
1. In a blender, blend together applesauce, caramel syrup, and cinnamon. Add in vodka, lime juice, and orange juice and blend until mixture is smooth.
2. Divide evenly into four glasses and serve.

Nutrition Information (per serving):
126 calories, 0 g fat, 15.2 g carbohydrates, 0 g protein.

2. Mediterranean Nicoise Salad

Mediterranean Nicoise Salad is a bright and colorful dish that combines a variety of flavors and textures. Perfect for a light meal or as a side, this salad is sure to add a touch of Mediterannean charm to your table!

Serving: 4 | Preparation Time: 20 minutes | Ready Time: 20 minutes

Ingredients:
-2 (5-ounce) cans tuna, drained
-3/4 cup green beans, parboiled
-3 small tomatoes, cubed
-1/2 cup black, pitted olives

-2 hard-boiled eggs, quartered
-2 tablespoons red wine vinegar
-2 tablespoons extra-virgin olive oil
-Salt and freshly cracked pepper, to taste

Instructions:
1. In a medium bowl, combine tuna, green beans, tomatoes, olives, and eggs, and set aside.
2. In a small bowl, whisk together red wine vinegar, olive oil, salt, and pepper and pour over the salad.
3. Mix everything together until all the ingredients are evenly coated.
4. Serve chilled.

Nutrition Information:
Calories: 165 kcal / serving, Protein: 18g / serving, Fat: 10g / serving, Carbohydrates: 3g / serving, Sodium: 270mg / serving

3. Avocado Nicoise Salad

Avocado Nicoise Salad is a delicious and healthy dish made of crunchy lettuce and topped with seared tuna and potatoes, ripe avocados and a zesty vinaigrette. This salad is the perfect way to enjoy fresh, seasonal ingredients that deliver a satisfyingly balanced meal. The combination of flavors, textures and colors make this an exciting and uplifting dish.

Serving: 4 | Preparation Time: 15 minutes | Ready Time: 15 minutes

Ingredients:
• 4 cups of Romaine Lettuce, chopped
• 2 ripe avocados, thinly sliced
• 6 red potatoes, boiled and sliced
• 2 cans of tuna, seared
• 1/4 cup of fresh parsley, finely chopped
• 2 tablespoons of olive oil
• 2 tablespoons of white wine vinegar
• Salt and pepper to taste

Instructions:
1. Heat a skillet over medium heat and add the tuna. Sauté the tuna for 2-3 minutes until it's lightly browned.
2. In a large bowl, combine the Romaine lettuce, avocados, potatoes, and parsley.
3. In a small bowl, combine the olive oil, white wine vinegar, salt and pepper. Whisk to combine.
4. Add the dressing to the salad and toss to coat evenly.
5. Divide the salad among 4 plates, then top with the seared tuna.

Nutrition Information:
Calories Per Serving: 382 calories
Total Fat: 19 grams
Saturated Fat: 3 grams
Sodium: 545 milligrams
Carbohydrate: 35 grams
Fiber: 8.2 grams
Protein: 19 grams

4. Grilled Vegetable Nicoise Salad

Grilled Vegetable Nicoise Salad is a light, healthy summer salad featuring grilled vegetables, potatoes, and a zesty dressing. It's perfect for a light lunch or dinner served with crusty bread.

Servings: 4 | Preparation Time: 15 minutes | Ready Time: 15 minutes

Ingredients:
- 2 large potatoes
- 1 red pepper
- 1 zucchini
- 2 tablespoons olive oil
- 2 plum tomatoes, sliced in half
- 1 red onion, cut into wedges
- 1 head romaine lettuce, torn into bite-sized pieces
- 2 tablespoons capers
- 8 anchovy fillets, chopped
- 2 tablespoons freshly squeezed lemon juice

- Salt and freshly ground black pepper

Instructions:
1. Preheat the grill to high heat.
2. Dice the potatoes into small cubes and place in a medium bowl. Add the red pepper and zucchini and toss with the olive oil. Spread the vegetables onto the preheated grill and cook until lightly charred and cooked through.
3. Place the lettuce into a large bowl. Arrange the grilled vegetables on top, along with the tomatoes, red onion and capers.
4. In a small bowl, mix together the lemon juice and anchovy fillets and pour over the salad. Season with salt and pepper to taste.

Nutrition Information:
Per serving: 150 calories, 10 g fat, 4 g saturated fat, 25 mg cholesterol, 11 g carbohydrates, 4 g sugar, 5 g protein, 309 mg sodium, 4 g dietary fiber.

5. Roasted Butternut Squash Nicoise Salad

This Roasted Butternut Squash Nicoise Salad is an exquisite mix of roasted butternut squash, potatoes, green beans, olives, eggs and flavorful dressing. Perfect as a light lunch or dinner, this salad is sure to please.

Serving: 4 | Preparation Time: 20 minutes | Ready Time: 40 minutes

Ingredients:
- 1 large butternut squash, cut into cubes
- 1 pound new potatoes, cut into 1-inch cubes
- 2 tablespoons olive oil
- 1/2 teaspoon salt
- 1/4 teaspoon freshly ground black pepper
- 1 pound green beans, trimmed and halved
- 1/4 cup Nicoise olives
- 2 large eggs, hard boiled and cut into wedges
- 2 tablespoons Dijon mustard
- 2 tablespoons white balsamic vinegar
- 1 tablespoon honey

- 1/4 cup extra-virgin olive oil

Instructions:
1. Preheat the oven to 375F (190°C).
2. On a large baking sheet, toss the butternut squash and potatoes with the olive oil, salt, and pepper. Roast in the preheated oven for 20 minutes, stirring once or twice.
3. Meanwhile, bring a large pot of salted water to a boil over high heat. Add the green beans and cook until just tender, 3 to 4 minutes. Drain and rinse with cold water to stop the cooking.
4. In a large bowl, combine the roasted vegetables, green beans, olives, eggs and toss together.
5. In a small bowl, whisk together the Dijon mustard, white balsamic vinegar, honey and olive oil. Pour over the salad and toss to coat.
6. Serve.

Nutrition Information:
Serving Size (1/4 of recipe):
Calories: 250, Fat: 12g, Carbs: 32g, Protein: 6g

6. Cucumber Nicoise Salad

Cucumber Nicoise Salad is a hearty, Mediterranean-style dish loaded with fresh ingredients, bursting with flavor and perfect for any occasion.

Serves 4-6; | Preparation Time 10 minutes; Ready Time 10 minutes.

Ingredients:
- 2 English cucumbers, seeded and sliced
- 1 can (14.5 ounces) whole black olives, drained
- 1 red onion, diced small
- 1 cup cherry tomatoes, halved
- 2 tablespoons olive oil
- 2 tablespoons red wine vinegar
- 1/2 cup chopped fresh parsley
- Salt and black pepper, to taste

Instructions:
1. In a large bowl, combine the cucumbers, olives, red onion, and cherry tomatoes.
2. In a small bowl, whisk together the olive oil, red wine vinegar, and parsley until combined.
3. Pour the dressing over the cucumber mixture and toss to combine.
4. Season with salt and black pepper, to taste.

Nutrition Information (per serving):
128 calories; 9.5 g fat; 5.5 g carbohydrates; 2.5 g protein; 4.5 g fiber.

7. Nicoise Salad with Fried Egg

This delectable salad is a hearty combination of crisp vegetables, salty tuna, and a runny fried egg that's sure to please as a light lunch or outdoor meal.

Serving: 4-6 | Preparation Time: approximately 15 minutes | Ready Time: approximately 20 minutes

Ingredients:
- 1/4 cup olive oil
- 1/4 teaspoon Dijon mustard
- 2 tablespoons red wine vinegar
- 4 cups mixed greens
- 2 cups grape tomatoes, halved
- 1/2 cup pitted kalamata olives
- 1/2 cup artichoke hearts, drained
- 1/4 cup capers
- 1 (5-ounce) can chunk light tuna, rinsed and drained
- 1/2 teaspoon freshly ground black pepper
- 2 fried eggs

Instructions:
1. In a medium bowl, combine the olive oil, mustard, and red wine vinegar and whisk to combine.

2. In a large bowl, combine the mixed greens, tomatoes, olives, artichokes, capers, and tuna.
3. Drizzle the dressing over the salad and toss to combine.
4. Divide the salad among four plates. Sprinkle the pepper over each plate.
5. Top each plate with a fried egg.

Nutrition Information:
Per Serving:
Calories: 309
Carbs: 17 g
Protein: 11 g
Fat: 22 g
Cholesterol: 186 mg

8. Nicoise Salad with Tuna

Nicoise Salad with Tuna is a classic salad that includes some of the best flavors of the Mediterranean. The combination of flavorful tuna, fresh greens, and a light vinaigrette dressing make this salad a delight.

Serving: 4 | Preparation Time: 15 mins | Ready Time: 15 mins

Ingredients:
- 2 cans of tuna,
- 6-7 hard boiled eggs,
- 4-5 potatoes,
- 4-5 tomatoes,
- 1 cup of green beans,
- 1 cup of olives,
- 1 cup of vinaigrette dressing

Instructions:
- Begin by boiling the potatoes and eggs until tender, about 10 minutes. Let cool and slice into bite-sized pieces.
- Slice the tomatoes and mix together in a large bowl with the beans, tuna, olives, and potatoes.

- Drizzle the vinaigrette dressing over the salad and thoroughly mix it together.
- Serve chilled on a bed of lettuce or other fresh greens.

Nutrition Information:
Calories: 375, Protein: 19.6g, Total Fat: 17.7g, Saturated Fat: 2g, Cholesterol: 148.3mg, Sodium: 517.3mg, Carbohydrates: 28.7g, Fiber: 5.8g, Sugars: 8.4g.

9. Nicoise Salad with Shrimp

This Nicoise Salad with Shrimp is an elegant, light and flavorful dish that is perfect for a summertime meal. It is an ideal mix of crunchy greens, sweet shrimp, and savory olives, tomatoes, and artichokes. Serve this salad with a light vinaigrette for a perfect summer salad.

Servings: 4 | Preparation Time: 20 minutes | Ready Time: 20 minutes

Ingredients:
• 4 cups mixed greens
• 4 frozen cooked shrimp pieces
• 10 cherry tomatoes, halved
• 3 tablespoons sliced black olives
• 2 tablespoons chopped artichoke hearts
• 2 tablespoons extra-virgin olive oil
• 2 teaspoons red wine vinegar
• 1/2 teaspoon minced garlic
• Salt and pepper

Instructions:
1. Place the mixed greens in a large bowl.
2. Add the shrimp, tomatoes, olives and artichoke hearts.
3. In a small bowl, whisk together the olive oil, vinegar, garlic, salt, and pepper.
4. Pour over the salad and gently toss to combine.
5. Serve immediately.

Nutrition Information:
• Calories: 191
• Fat: 11g
• Cholesterol: 58 mg
• Sodium: 107 mg
• Carbohydrates: 9g
• Protein: 12g

10. Nicoise Salad with Olives

Nicoise Salad with Olives is a French classic that combines ripe tomatoes, crunchy cucumbers, boiled eggs, crisp greens, tuna, and olives in a vibrant vinaigrette. This delicious and hearty salad is a perfect meal for any occasion.

Serving: 4-6 | Preparation Time: 25 minutes | Ready Time: 25 minutes

Ingredients:
-3 tablespoons red wine vinegar
-1 tablespoon Dijon mustard
-1/4 cup extra-virgin olive oil
-Salt and pepper
-2 heads romaine lettuce, torn into bite-sized pieces
-1 pint cherry tomatoes, halved
-1 cucumber, peeled, seeded and diced
-2 boiled eggs, peeled and quartered
-1 (7-ounce) can tuna, drained and flaked
-2 tablespoons chopped fresh parsley
-1/3 cup pitted Nicoise olives

Instructions:
1. In a medium bowl, whisk together the vinegar, mustard, olive oil, salt and pepper.
2. In a large bowl, combine the lettuce, tomatoes, cucumber, eggs, tuna, parsley and olives.
3. Pour the dressing over the salad and toss to combine.
4. Divide the salad among individual plates and serve.

Nutrition Information:
Calories: 287; Protein: 15g; Total Fat: 19g; Saturated Fat: 3g; Cholesterol: 88mg; Carbohydrates: 12g; Fiber: 4g; Sugar: 5g; Sodium: 517mg

11. Nicoise Salad with Baby Potatoes

Nicoise Salad with Baby Potatoes is a classic French salad featuring protein-packed boiled eggs, blanched green beans, and Little Potatoes. The simple dressing of olive oil, garlic, and lemon brightens up the flavors of the vegetables and potatoes. This salad provides a delicious, nutritious and colorful meal.

Serving: 4 | Preparation Time: 20 minutes | Ready Time: 20 minutes

Ingredients:
- 8 ounces Little Potatoes
- 2 tablespoons olive oil
- 2 tablespoons red wine vinegar
- 1 teaspoon fresh lemon juice
- 2 cloves of garlic, minced
- 2 hard-boiled eggs, cut into wedges
- 4 ounces green beans, blanched
- 1 cup cherry tomatoes, halved
- 2 tablespoons capers
- Salt and pepper, to taste

Instructions:
1. Place Little Potatoes in a steamer and steam for 10 minutes.
2. Meanwhile, combine olive oil, red wine vinegar, lemon juice, garlic, salt, and pepper in a bowl, whisking to combine.
3. In a separate salad bowl, combine potatoes, eggs, green beans, tomatoes and capers.
4. Pour dressing over salad and toss to combine.

Nutrition Information (per serving):
Calories: 101; Total Fat: 6.3 g; Cholesterol: 68.5 mg; Sodium: 115.6 mg; Total Carbohydrates: 7.3 g; Dietary Fiber: 2.1 g; Protein: 3.9 g

12. Nicoise Salad with Artichoke Hearts

Nicoise Salad with Artichoke Hearts is an easy yet tasty Mediterranean-inspired salad that combines flavorful vegetables with the clean taste of artichoke hearts. It's perfect for lunch, dinner, or even a light weeknight meal.

Serving: 4-6 | Preparation Time: 20 minutes | Ready Time: 20 minutes

Ingredients:
- 4 cups chopped romaine lettuce
- 1 (14 ounces) can quartered artichoke hearts, drained
- 1 red bell pepper, cored and chopped
- 1/2 cup halved cherry tomatoes
- 1/4 cup diced red onion
- 1/4 cup sliced black olives, chopped
- 4 tablespoons olive oil
- 1 tablespoon red wine vinegar
- salt and pepper to taste

Instructions:
1. In a large salad bowl, combine the lettuce, artichoke hearts, red bell pepper, cherry tomatoes, red onion, and olives.
2. In a small bowl, whisk together the olive oil and red wine vinegar.
3. Drizzle the dressing over the salad and toss to combine.
4. Season with salt and pepper to taste.

Nutrition Information:
Serving size (1/6 of the salad): Calories 138, Total Fat 8.8g, Saturated Fat 1.3g, Cholesterol 0mg, Sodium 213.7mg, Total Carbohydrates 12.2g, Dietary Fiber 4.2g, Protein 4.1g.

13. Nicoise Salad with Roasted Red Peppers

Nicoise Salad with Roasted Red Peppers is a hearty and flavorful entrée that is perfect for a light lunch or dinner. This salad has the perfect balance of fresh greens, olives, roasted red peppers and tuna that make it a delightful dish.

Serving: Makes 4 servings | Preparation Time: 15 minutes | Ready Time: 15 minutes

Ingredients:
- 2 hearts romaine lettuce, washed and chopped into bite-sized pieces
- 2 cans of tuna in olive oil, drained and flaked
- 4 roasted red peppers, sliced into thin strips
- 2 garlic cloves, minced
- 1/2 cup black olives
- 1/4 cup olive oil
- Juice of 1 lemon
- 2 tablespoons red wine vinegar
- Salt and pepper to taste

Instructions:
1. In a large bowl, combine the romaine lettuce, tuna, roasted red peppers, garlic and olives.
2. In a separate bowl, whisk together the olive oil, lemon juice, red wine vinegar, salt and pepper.
3. Pour the dressing over the salad and toss everything to combine.
4. Serve the salad chilled or at room temperature.

Nutrition Information:
Calories 185; Total fat 10.8g; Saturated fat 1.51g; Sodium 188.4 mg; Carbohydrates 11.4g; Fiber 3.31g; Sugar 1.7g; Protein 15.4g.

14. Nicoise Salad with Feta Cheese

This Nicoise Salad with Feta Cheese is a fresh, colorful take on the classic French dish, with a zesty dressing. It's packed with protein from tuna and beans and full of flavor from feta cheese, olives, and herbs. Serve as a side or light meal – it's perfect for any occasion.

Serving: 6-8 | Preparation Time: 10 minutes | Ready Time: 10 minutes

Ingredients:
- 4 tbsp. extra virgin olive oil
- 2 tbsp. red wine vinegar

- 2 cloves garlic, minced
- 1/2 teaspoon sea salt
- 1/4 teaspoon freshly-ground black pepper
- 2 cans (5 ounces each) tuna, drained
- 2 cups cooked green beans
- 1 head romaine lettuce, washed and chopped
- 1/2 cup black olives, pitted and halved
- 1/2 cup tomato, diced
- 1/2 cup feta cheese, crumbled
- 2 tablespoons chopped fresh parsley, for garnish

Instructions:
1. In a medium bowl, whisk together the olive oil, red wine vinegar, garlic, salt, and pepper.
2. Gently fold in the tuna, green beans, romaine, olives, tomatoes, and feta cheese.
3. Gently toss to combine, then sprinkle with chopped parsley.
4. Serve chilled.

Nutrition Information:
calories: 170
protein: 11 g
fat: 9 g
carbohydrates: 8 g
sodium: 263 mg

15. Nicoise Salad with Sun-Dried Tomatoes

Nicoise Salad with Sun-Dried Tomatoes is an exquisite and flavorful salad. Packed with fresh vegetables, succulent olives, and a marinated tomato dressing, this delicious salad is perfect for summer gatherings or as a light lunch.

Serving: 4 | Preparation Time: 20 minutes | Ready Time: 20 minutes

Ingredients:
- 2 heads romaine lettuce, cut into 1-inch pieces
- 1/2 cup torn fresh basil leaves

- 1/2 cup sun-dried tomatoes, chopped
- 1/2 cup kalamata olives
- 1/2 cup crumbled feta cheese
- 2 tablespoons olive oil
- 2 tablespoons balsamic vinegar
- 1/4 teaspoon sea salt

Instructions:
1. In a large bowl, combine the lettuce, basil, sun-dried tomatoes, olives, and feta cheese.
2. In a small bowl, whisk together the olive oil, balsamic vinegar, and salt.
3. Drizzle the dressing over the salad and toss to combine.
4. Serve immediately.

Nutrition Information:
• Calories: 140
• Fat: 10g
• Carbs: 10g
• Protein: 2g

16. Nicoise Salad with Prosciutto

Nicoise Salad with Prosciutto is a unique, flavorful and delicious salad that will make a great side dish to your favorite entrée. This traditional French recipe combines salty prosciutto and classic Nicoise ingredients, making a nutritious meal that will tantalize your taste buds.

Serving: 4-6 | Preparation Time: 15 minutes | Ready Time: 15 minutes

Ingredients:
- 8-10 ounces of prosciutto, thinly sliced
- 2 medium sized red potatoes, diced
- 6 cups of Romaine lettuce, chopped
- 1/4 red onion, thinly sliced
- 1 pint cherry tomatoes, halved
- 1 can of tuna in olive oil, drained
- 1/2 cup Niçoise olives
- 1/4 cup extra-virgin olive oil

- 2 tablespoons freshly squeezed lemon juice
- Salt & freshly ground black pepper to taste

Instructions:
1. Bring a pot of salted water to a boil and add the diced potatoes. Cook for about 5 minutes or until just tender. Quickly put the potatoes in cold water to stop the cooking process.
2. In a large bowl, combine the Romaine lettuce, red onion and cherry tomatoes.
3. Add the cooked potatoes, tuna and Niçoise olives.
4. Pour in the extra-virgin olive oil and lemon juice, then season with salt and pepper to taste.
5. Top the salad with the thinly sliced prosciutto.

Nutrition Information:
For a 1-cup serving, Nicoise Salad with Prosciutto contains approximately 107 calories, 7.5 grams of fat, 9.5 grams of carbohydrates, and 342 mg of sodium.

17. Nicoise Salad with Capers

Nicoise Salad with Capers is a fresh and vibrant salad that comes together in just minutes. A combination of tomatoes, olives, eggs, bell peppers, capers, and tuna, this salad packs a flavorful punch and is finished off with a classic vinaigrette. This salad is perfect for a light lunch or a side dish for dinner.

Serving: 4 | Preparation Time: 15 minutes | Ready Time: 15 minutes

Ingredients:
- 4 tablespoons olive oil
- 1 tablespoons white wine vinegar
- 2 shallots, finely diced
- 1 garlic clove, minced
- 2 tablespoons of capers
- 2 large tomatoes, cut into wedges
- 1 bell pepper, julienned
- 2 hard boiled eggs, quartered

- 1 6-ounce can of tuna, drained
- 1/2 cup black olives
- 1/4 cup parsley, finely chopped
- Salt and pepper to taste

Instructions:
1. In a small bowl, whisk together the olive oil, white wine vinegar, shallots, garlic, and capers.
2. In a large bowl, combine the tomatoes, bell pepper, eggs, tuna, olives, and parsley.
3. Pour in the vinaigrette and gently toss to combine.
4. Season with salt and pepper to taste.
5. Serve immediately or store in the refrigerator.

Nutrition Information:
Calories: 259 kcal, Carbohydrates: 8 g, Protein: 14 g, Fat: 18 g, Saturated Fat: 3 g, Cholesterol: 67 mg, Sodium: 498 mg, Potassium: 465 mg, Fiber: 3 g, Sugar: 4 g, Vitamin A: 300 IU, Vitamin C: 40 mg, Calcium: 51 mg, Iron: 2 mg

18. Nicoise Salad with Sweet Potatoes

An Nicoise Salad with Sweet Potatoes is a flavorful and nutritious twist on the traditional Nicoise Salad. This salad is perfect for a light and refreshing summer meal, and it's sure to please the whole family. Serve this salad up with your favorite salad dressings and enjoy!

Serving: 4-6 | Preparation Time: 10 minutes | Ready Time: 15 minutes

Ingredients:
• 2 sweet potatoes, diced and cooked
• 4 cups lettuce mix
• 4 hard boiled eggs, chopped
• 1/2 cup kalamata olives
• 1/2 cup cherry tomatoes, halved
• 1/2 cup cooked green beans
• 2 tablespoons extra-virgin olive oil
• 2 tablespoons red wine vinegar

• Salt and black pepper, to taste

Instructions:
1. In a large bowl, combine all of the ingredients.
2. Drizzle with extra- virgin olive oil and red wine vinegar.
3. Season with salt and black pepper, to taste.
4. Mix all ingredients until combined.
5. Serve chilled or at room temperature.

Nutrition Information (per serving):
Calories: 154 kcal, Protein: 7 g, Fat: 8 g, Carbohydrates: 14 g, Fiber: 3 g, Sodium: 173 mg

19. Nicoise Salad with Warm Bacon

Nicoise Salad with Warm Bacon is a delectable dish with a combination of salty and smoky bacon, fresh vegetables, and a delicious dressing. Each bite has a delightful mix of flavors and textures.

Serving: 4 | Preparation Time: 15 minutes | Ready Time: 25 minutes

Ingredients:
- 4 slices of bacon
- 2 heads of romaine lettuce, washed and chopped
- 2 hard boiled eggs, halved
- 1 red bell pepper, sliced
- 1 cup cherry or grape tomatoes, halved
- 1/4 cup kalamata olives, pitted
- 2 tablespoons olive oil
- 1 tablespoon white wine vinegar
- 2 teaspoons Dijon mustard
- Salt and pepper to taste

Instruction:
1. Preheat the oven to 400 F. Lay the bacon slices on a parchment-lined baking sheet and bake for 10-15 minutes until crispy.
2. In a medium bowl, toss together the lettuce, eggs, bell pepper, tomatoes, and olives.

3. In a separate small bowl, whisk together the olive oil, vinegar, and mustard. Pour the dressing over the salad and toss gently.
4. Place the salad on four plates and top with crumbled bacon. Season with salt and pepper, to taste.

Nutrition Information (per serving):
251 calories, 22g fat, 8g carbohydrate, 7g protein

20. Nicoise Salad with Anchovies

Nicoise Salad with Anchovies is a French classic dish made with healthy ingredients, like tomatoes, potatoes, green beans, and anchovies. This salad is great for a light meal or lunch and is surprisingly easy to make.

Serving: 4-6 | Preparation Time: 15 minutes | Ready Time: 15 minutes

Ingredients:
- 4-6 anchovy fillets
- 2-3 tomatoes, diced
- 2-3 potatoes, boiled and diced
- 1 can of green beans, drained
- 2-3 tablespoons of olive oil
- 2-3 tablespoons of red vinegar
- Salt and pepper to taste

Instructions:
1. In a medium serving bowl, combine the anchovies and potato.
2. Add tomatoes, green beans and mix together.
3. Drizzle olive oil and red vinegar over the mixture and season with salt and pepper.
4. Mix to combine.
5. Serve cold, as is or with a light vinaigrette.

Nutrition Information:
Calories: 200 *
Fat: 6g
Carbohydrates: 25 g
Protein: 8g

Nutrition Information:
Based on ingredients and may vary.

21. Nicoise Salad with Avocado and Grapefruit

Nicoise Salad with Avocado and Grapefruit is the perfect hearty and healthy dish for any meal! This salad has a zesty dressing that brings out the sweetness of grapefruit, plus the added crunch from the vegetables and nutty flavour from the proteins. It's a great way to get your day started or a lovely light lunch.

Serving: 4 | Preparation Time: 10 minutes | Ready Time: 20 minutes

Ingredients:
- 2 avocados, sliced
- 2 grapefruit, peeled and segmented
- 1 head of romaine lettuce, chopped
- 1/2 cup of almonds, toasted and chopped
- 1/2 cup feta cheese, crumbled
- 1/2 cup black olives
- 4 eggs, hard-boiled and quartered
- 2 tablespoons fresh dill, chopped
- 2 tablespoons olive oil
- 1 teaspoon lemon juice
- Salt and pepper, to taste

Instructions:
1. In a large bowl, toss together the romaine lettuce, almonds, feta cheese, olives, eggs, and dill.
2. In a small bowl, whisk together the olive oil, lemon juice, and salt and pepper. Pour the dressing over the salad and toss to combine.
3. Top the salad with the avocado and grapefruit segments and serve.

Nutrition Information:
Calories: 390, Fat: 26 g, Carbohydrates: 19 g, Protein: 16 g, Fiber: 8 g, Cholesterol: 172 mg

22. Nicoise Salad with Mozzarella

Nicoise Salad With Mozzarella is an easy yet delicious salad that is sure to be a crowd-pleaser. Combining flavorful tuna and colorful veggies with a creamy mozzarella cheese, this salad is a healthier twist on the classic Nicoise salad.

Serving: 4 | Preparation Time: 10 minutes | Ready Time: 15 minutes

Ingredients:
- 4 cups mixed salad greens
- 2 cans tuna in water
- 1 16 oz can of artichoke hearts in water, drained and chopped
- 1/4 cup pitted black olives
- 1/3 cup cherry tomatoes, halved
- 8 oz. fresh mozzarella, cut into cubes
- 2 tablespoons olive oil
- 2 tablespoons red wine vinegar
- 1 tablespoon minced garlic
- Salt and pepper to taste

Instructions:
1. In a large bowl, combine the salad greens, tuna, artichoke hearts, olives, and tomatoes.
2. In a separate bowl, whisk together the olive oil, vinegar, garlic, salt and pepper.
3. Drizzle the dressing over the salad and toss to combine.
4. Top the salad with the fresh mozzarella cubes.
5. Serve cold and enjoy!

Nutrition Information:
Calories: 277 kcal, Carbohydrates: 9g, Protein: 21g, Fat: 16g, Saturated Fat: 4g, Cholesterol: 39mg, Sodium: 474mg, Potassium: 455mg, Fiber: 4g, Sugar: 4g, Vitamin A: 1943IU, Vitamin C: 29mg, Calcium: 288mg, Iron: 1mg

23. Nicoise Salad with Quinoa

This unique twist on the traditional Niçoise salad combines nutritious quinoa with classic ingredients like tomatoes, olives, and eggs. It's a delicious and healthy dish perfect for lunch, dinner, or a simple side dish.

Serving: 4-6 | Preparation Time: 10 minutes | Ready Time: 25 minutes

Ingredients:
- 1 cup of cooked quinoa
- 2 cups of cherry or grape tomatoes, halved
- 2 cups of cooked green beans
- 1/2 cup of pitted kalamata olives
- 2 hard boiled eggs, chopped
- 4-6 tablespoons of extra-virgin olive oil
- 4 tablespoons of red wine vinegar
- 1 teaspoon of Dijon mustard
- Salt and pepper, to taste

Instruction:
1. Cook the quinoa according to the package instructions. Set aside to cool.
2. In a large bowl, combine the tomatoes, green beans, olives, and eggs.
3. In a small bowl, whisk together the olive oil, vinegar, mustard, salt, and pepper. Pour over the salad and mix to combine.
4. Add the cooked quinoa to the bowl and stir to combine.
5. Serve.

Nutrition Information: per serve:
290 kcal, Fat 19g, Carbs 21g, Protein 8g

24. Nicoise Salad with Edamame

Nicoise Salad with Edamame is a tasty and healthy dish featuring fresh vegetables artfully combined with edamame and dressed in classic vinaigrette. This recipe yields 4 servings, takes 10 minutes to prepare and 10 minutes to cook and offers nutritional benefits thanks to the nutrient-rich edamame.

Serving: 4 | Preparation Time: 10 minutes | Ready Time: 10 minutes

Ingredients:
- 2 cups edamame, shelled and cooked
- 1 large head of romaine lettuce, chopped
- 1 large tomato, diced
- 1 red onion, sliced
- 1 red bell pepper, diced
- 1/2 cup black olives, pitted and sliced
- 1/4 cup extra-virgin olive oil
- 2 tablespoons red wine vinegar
- Salt and pepper, to taste

Instructions:
1. In a large salad bowl, combine the edamame, romaine lettuce, tomato, red onion, bell pepper and black olives.
2. In a small bowl, whisk together the olive oil, red wine vinegar and a pinch of salt and pepper.
3. Drizzle the vinaigrette over the salad and toss to combine.
4. Divide the salad between 4 plates and serve.

Nutrition Information:
Calories: 208, Fat: 13.7g, Cholesterol: 0mg, Sodium: 303.2mg, Carbohydrates: 15.4g, Protein: 10.4g

25. Nicoise Salad with Beets

Nicoise Salad with Beets is a delightful summer salad that is packed full of bright, vibrant flavors. Beets, olives, potatoes, cucumbers, and hard boiled eggs come together with a simple vinaigrette dressing to make this delicious and nutritious salad.

Serving: 4 | Preparation Time: 20 minutes | Ready Time: 20 minutes

Ingredients:
- 4 beets (roasted, peeled, and diced)
- 2 cups small potatoes (boiled and quartered)
- 1 large cucumber (diced)

- 1/2 cup pickled olives
- 2 hard boiled eggs (chopped)
- 2 tablespoons extra-virgin olive oil
- 2 tablespoons red wine vinegar
- 2 tablespoons Dijon mustard
- Salt and pepper

Instructions:
1. Prepare the beets for the salad by washing, peeling, and roasting.
2. Boil the potatoes in a pot of salted water for 10 minutes. Drain and allow to cool before cutting into quarters.
3. Toss the diced beets, potatoes, cucumber, and olives in a bowl.
4. In a separate bowl, whisk together the olive oil, red wine vinegar, and Dijon mustard.
5. Pour the dressing over the salad, and toss to combine.
6. Top with chopped hard boiled eggs and season with salt and pepper.
7. Serve and enjoy!

Nutrition Information:
Calories: 300, Fat: 10 g, Carbohydrates: 36 g, Protein: 8 g, Sodium: 585 mg, Fiber: 5 g

26. Nicoise Salad with Scallops

Nicoise Salad with Scallops is a delicious, light and healthy meal, perfect for spring and summer evenings. This dish combines tender scallops, fresh greens and a light vinaigrette made with white wine and shallots for a truly flavorful meal.

Serving: 4 servings | Preparation Time: 15 minutes | Ready Time: 15 minutes

Ingredients:
• 8 Large Sea Scallops
• 2 Cups Mesclun Greens
• 1/4 Red Onion, thinly sliced
• 1 Carrot, julienned
• 1 Celery Stalk, julienned

- 2 Hard-boiled Eggs, quartered
- 6 Cherry Tomatoes, halved
- 1/4 Cup White Wine Vinegar
- 2 Tablespoons Extra Virgin Olive Oil
- 1/2 Shallot, minced
- 1/2 Teaspoon Dijon Mustard
- 2 Tablespoons Chopped Fresh Parsley
- Salt and Freshly Ground Black Pepper to taste

Instructions:
1. Heat a greased or non-sticking pan over medium-high heat.
2. Cook the scallops for 2-3 minutes on each side, or until they are lightly golden.
3. Meanwhile, in a large bowl, combine the mesclun greens, red onion, carrot, celery, eggs, and tomatoes.
4. In a small bowl, whisk together the vinegar, olive oil, shallot, mustard, parsley, salt, and pepper.
5. Pour the dressing over the salad and toss to combine.
6. Place the salad on a serving platter and top with the cooked scallops.
7. Serve immediately.

Nutrition Information:
- Per Serving: 300 calories; 16g fat; 14g carbohydrates; 16g protein; 300mg sodium.

27. Nicoise Salad with Asparagus

A Nicoise Salad with Asparagus is a classic French salad made with tuna, hard boiled eggs, potatoes, olives, tomatoes, and a light vinaigrette dressing. This salad is packed with flavor and is an excellent source of protein, making it perfect for a light meal.

Servings: 4 | Preparation Time: 20 minutes | Ready Time: 40 minutes

Ingredients:
- 3x5oz cans tuna in olive oil, drained
- 2 cups steamed asparagus
- 2 cups halved boiled potatoes

- 8 cherry tomatoes, halved
- 1 red onion, diced
- 1/4 cup Kalamata olives
- 4 large hard boiled eggs, quartered
- 1 cup vinaigrette dressing

Instructions:
1. Begin by steaming the 2 cups of asparagus in a large pot with approximately one inch of water. Allow to cook for 6-8 minutes.
2. Once cooked, drain and rinse the asparagus to cool.
3. Halve the boiled potatoes and add to a large bowl with the tuna, onion, tomatoes, olives, and asparagus.
4. Toss the ingredients with the vinaigrette dressing and season with salt and pepper to taste.
5. Place the salad onto plates and top with quartered boiled eggs.
6. Serve and enjoy!

Nutrition Information Per Serving:
Calories: 304, Fat: 15.0g, Saturated Fat: 2.4g, Protein: 21.1g, Carbohydrates: 19.1g, Sugar: 1.4g, Sodium: 545.0mg

28. Nicoise Salad with Poached Egg

Nicoise Salad with Poached Egg is a delicious and nutritious French salad recipe. It is a combination of tuna, eggs, green beans and potatoes, all dressed in a tasty vinaigrette. This salad is perfect to make in bulk, as it's versatile and can be enjoyed as a light lunch or dinner in fewer than 45 minutes!

Serving: 4 | Preparation Time: 10 minutes | Ready Time: 35 minutes

Ingredients:
- 4 potatoes, boiled and quartered
- 4 eggs
- 1 can tuna
- 2 handfuls of green beans, steamed
- 2 tablespoons of capers
- 250 ml olive oil

- 2 tablespoons red wine vinegar
- 2 tablespoons sugar
- 2 tablespoons fresh parsley, minced
- Salt and pepper, to taste

Instructions:
1. Bring a medium pot of water to a boil and add the quartered potatoes. Cook for 10 minutes, or until the potatoes are cooked but still firm.
2. Meanwhile, poach the eggs in a separate pot of boiling water for 3 to 5 minutes.
3. In a large bowl, combine the potatoes, tuna, green beans, capers, olive oil, red wine vinegar, sugar, parsley, and salt and pepper.
4. Divide the salad among four plates and top with a poached egg.

Nutrition Information:
- Calories: 298
- Total Fat: 22g
- Saturated Fat: 3g
- Sodium: 308mg
- Potassium: 446mg
- Total Carbohydrates: 16g
- Dietary Fiber: 3g
- Protein: 11g
- Vitamin A: 5.6%
- Vitamin C: 24.4%
- Calcium: 4.4%
- Iron: 15%

29. Nicoise Salad with Radishes

Nicoise Salad with Radishes is a delicious, healthy, and easy to make summer salad everyone is sure to love. This salad combines radishes, Romaine lettuce, tomatoes, cucumbers, hard boiled eggs, and olives to create a nutrient-filled meal.

Servings: 4 | Preparation Time: 15 minutes | Ready Time: 15 minutes

Ingredients:
- 2 heads romaine lettuce, chopped
- 10 radishes, sliced
- 2 tomatoes, diced
- 1 cucumber, chopped
- 4 hard boiled eggs, diced
- 1/2 cup black olives, halved
- 1/4 cup olive oil
- 2 tablespoons red wine vinegar
- Salt and freshly ground pepper

Instructions:
1. In a large bowl, combine romaine lettuce, radishes, tomatoes, cucumber, hard boiled eggs, and olives.
2. In a separate bowl, whisk together olive oil and red wine vinegar, and season to taste with salt and freshly ground pepper.
3. Drizzle dressing over salad and toss to combine.
4. Serve chilled.

Nutrition Information:
Per serving: Calories: 270; Fat: 16.8g; Carbohydrates: 16.5g; Protein: 11.8g; Sodium: 707mg; Fiber: 5.9g

30. Nicoise Salad with Arugula

Nicoise Salad with Arugula is a delicious and healthy meal that is packed with nutritious ingredients. This flavorful salad is a great way to get your quota of veggies in one go! It serves 4-5 people and can be prepared in 10 minutes and ready to serve in 15 minutes.

Serving: 4-5 people | Preparation Time: 10 minutes | Ready Time: 15 minutes

Ingredients:
- 5oz of Arugula
- 12oz of Tuna (In olive oil, drained)
- 1 Yellow Bell Pepper (Sliced)
- 10 Black Olives (Sliced)

- 4-5 Hard boiled Eggs (diced)
- 2 Tomatoes (Chopped)
- 1 Shallot (Minced)
- 2 cloves Garlic (Minced)
- 2tbsp Olive Oil
- 1tbsp Red Wine Vinegar
- 2tsp Dijon Mustard
- Salt and Pepper (To Taste)

Instructions:
1. Preheat the oven to 350 degrees Fahrenheit.
2. Place the sliced bell pepper onto a baking sheet and roast in the oven for 20 minutes.
3. In a large salad bowl, combine the Arugula, tuna, roasted bell pepper, olives, eggs, tomatoes, shallot, garlic, olive oil, red wine vinegar, dijon and mustard.
4. Toss the salad ingredients to combine.
5. Add salt and pepper to taste.
6. Serve immediately.

Nutrition Information:
Calories: 203, Total Fat: 13g, Saturated Fat: 2g, Sodium: 274mg
Carbohydrates: 5g, Protein: 14g

31. Nicoise Salad with Chickpeas

Nicoise Salad with Chickpeas is a flavorful and healthy Mediterranean recipe made with boiled eggs, tomatoes, potatoes, black olives, tuna, and green beans dressed with a garlic vinaigrette.

Serving: 4 | Preparation Time: 15 minutes | Ready Time: 15 minutes

Ingredients:
• 4 Hard-boiled Eggs
• 1 cup Cherry Tomatoes
• 2 Potatoes, boiled
• 8-10 Black Olives, sliced
• 2 6-ounce cans Tuna, drained

- 1/2 cup Green Beans, blanched
- 2 cloves Garlic, minced
- 1/4 cup Red Wine Vinegar
- 1 teaspoon Dijon Mustard
- 1/4 cup Olive Oil
- Salt and Pepper, to taste

Instructions:
1. Start by boiling the eggs, tomatoes, and potatoes. Also blanch the green beans.
2. Combine the red wine vinegar, Dijon mustard, garlic and olive oil to make a vinaigrette.
3. Arrange the boiled eggs, tomatoes, potatoes, black olives, tuna, and green beans and dress with the vinaigrette.
4. Season with salt and pepper and serve.

Nutrition Information (per serving):
326 Calories, 20.5g Fat, 12.5g Carbs, 18.2g Protein

32. Nicoise Salad with Green Beans

Nicoise Salad with Green Beans is a easy and delicious vegetable-based salad from the south of France. It brings together crunchy green beans and potatoes with salty olives and oil-packed tuna for an amazing flavor combination.

Serving: 4-6 | Preparation Time: 10 minutes | Ready Time: 10 minutes

Ingredients:
- 2 cups green beans, trimmed
- 2 potatoes, diced
- 1/2 cup olives, pitted and halved
- 4 Roma (plum) tomatoes, cut into wedges
- 2 cans tuna in oil, drained
- 2 tablespoons olive oil
- 2 tablespoons red wine vinegar
- 2 cloves garlic, minced
- Salt and pepper, to taste

- 1 tablespoon minced fresh parsley (optional)

Instructions:
1. Fill a large pot with water, and bring to a boil. Add green beans and cook for 4 minutes, or until crisp-tender. Drain, and let cool.
2. In the same pot, add potatoes and enough water to cover. Cook 10 minutes or until tender. Drain, and let cool.
3. In a large bowl, combine cooked green beans, potatoes, olives, tomatoes and tuna.
4. In a separate bowl, whisk together olive oil, vinegar, garlic, salt and pepper. Pour over salad and mix together.
5. Serve at room temperature, or chill for a few hours before serving. Sprinkle with parsley, if desired

Nutrition Information:
Calories: 225; Total Fat: 11.3g; Sodium: 420mg; Carbohydrates: 20.8g; Fiber: 5.3g; Protein: 11.8g

33. Nicoise Salad with Goat Cheese

Nicoise Salad with Goat Cheese is a delicious, French-inspired salad that features a variety of savory ingredients. The combination of mixed greens, tomatoes, potatoes, egg, olives, tuna, capers and creamy goat cheese makes this salad a gourmet delight.

Serving: 6 | Preparation Time: 15 minutes | Ready Time: 15 minutes

Ingredients:
- 2 cups mixed greens
- 2 large tomatoes, diced
- 2 potatoes, boiled and sliced
- 1 hardboiled egg, peeled and diced
- 1/2 cup olives, chopped
- 1 can tuna, drained
- 2 tablespoons capers
- 4 ounces goat cheese, crumbled
- 2 tablespoons olive oil
- 2 tablespoons red wine vinegar

- 1 tablespoon Dijon mustard
- Salt and pepper, to taste

Instructions:
1. In a large bowl, combine the mixed greens, diced tomatoes, boiled potatoes, diced egg, olives, tuna, and capers.
2. In a separate bowl, whisk together the olive oil, red wine vinegar, Dijon mustard, salt and pepper.
3. Pour the dressing over the salad and toss to combine.
4. Sprinkle the goat cheese over the salad, then serve.

Nutrition Information:
Calories: 224 | Fat: 12g | Carbs: 18g | Protein: 11g

34. Nicoise Salad with Roasted Garlic

Nicoise salad is a classic French-style salad that consists of fresh herbs, potatoes, tuna, beans and eggs dressed in a lightly herby dressing. This version adds roasted garlic to create an even richer and more robust flavor. Serve this salad as a light main or side dish.

Servings: 4 | Preparation Time: 15 minutes | Ready Time: 15 minutes

Ingredients:
- 2 large potatoes, peeled and diced
- 2 cans of tuna, drained
- 2 cups green beans, blanched and cooled
- 2 hard-boiled eggs, sliced
- 6 cloves of roasted garlic, minced
- 1/2 cup extra virgin olive oil
- 1 tbsp Dijon mustard
- Juice of 1/2 lemon
- 2 tbsp chopped parsley

Instructions:
1. Heat oven to 375F. Place garlic cloves in an oven-safe dish and roast for 12-15 minutes until golden and fragrant.

2. Cook potatoes in boiling salted water for 10 minutes until tender, then drain and cool.

3. In a small bowl, whisk together olive oil, mustard, lemon juice and parsley.

4. To assemble, combine potatoes, tuna, green beans, eggs and roasted garlic in a large bowl. Drizzle with dressing and toss gently to combine.

Nutrition Information:
Calories: 690 | Total Fat: 55g | Saturated Fat: 7g | Cholesterol: 123mg | Sodium: 288mg | Total Carbohydrates: 40g | Fiber: 10g | Protein: 24g

35. Nicoise Salad with Seared Tuna

Nicoise Salad with Seared Tuna is a delicious and healthy Mediterranean-style salad made with fresh tuna, mixed greens, crunchy vegetables, potatoes and hard boiled eggs. This salad is packed with flavor, texture and great nutrition. It is perfect for a light lunch or as a side salad for any occasion.

Serving: 4 | Preparation Time: 20 minutes | Ready Time: 20 minutes

Ingredients:
- 2 6-ounce cans tuna in olive oil, drained
- 2 tablespoons olive oil
- 1 teaspoon smoked paprika
- 4 cups of mixed greens
- 1 cup baby tomatoes, halved
- 1 small cucumber, cut into thin slices
- 1/2 red onion, thinly sliced
- 2 red potatoes, chopped into cubes and boiled
- 2 cloves garlic, minced
- 2 hard boiled eggs, quartered
- 2 tablespoons chopped fresh parsley
- 2 tablespoons chopped pitted kalamata olives
- 2 tablespoons balsamic vinegar
- 1 tablespoon capers
- Salt and pepper, to taste

Instructions:

1. Heat olive oil in a large skillet over medium heat.
2. Add the tuna, paprika, minced garlic, salt and pepper. Sear until golden and cooked through, about 4 minutes per side. Set aside and let cool.
3. In a large bowl, combine the mixed greens, tomatoes, cucumber, red onion and potatoes.
4. In a separate bowl, whisk together the balsamic vinegar, capers, parsley and olives.
5. Pour vinaigrette over the salad and toss gently to combine.
6. Top the salad with the seared tuna, hard boiled eggs and any additional seasoning, if desired.

Nutrition Information:
Per Serving: 280 calories; 14g fat; 14g carbohydrates; 20g protein.

36. Nicoise Salad with Lemon Basil Vinaigrette

This Nicoise Salad with Lemon Basil Vinaigrette is a tangy and flavorful salad that's perfect for a summer meal or brunch. It is easy to make and sure to be the star of the plate.

Serving: 8 | Preparation Time: 10 minutes | Ready Time: 15 minutes

Ingredients:
- 2-3 romaine hearts, diced
- 2 cups cherry tomatoes, halved
- 1 cup cooked green beans
- 2-3 boiled eggs, diced
- 1/2 cup kalamata olives, pitted
- 2-3 tablespoons Italian parsley, chopped
- 1 cup cooked tuna, diced
- 1/4 cup feta cheese, crumbled
- Salt and pepper to taste
- 1/4 cup extra-virgin olive oil
- 2 tablespoons lemon juice
- 1 tablespoon Dijon mustard
- 1/2 teaspoon honey
- 1 clove garlic, minced

- 2 tablespoons fresh basil, chopped

Instructions:
1. In a large bowl, combine the diced romaine hearts, cherry tomatoes, green beans, diced boiled eggs, olives, Italian parsley, tuna, and feta cheese. Season with salt and pepper.
2. To make the vinaigrette, whisk together the olive oil, lemon juice, Dijon mustard, honey, minced garlic, and fresh basil.
3. Drizzle the vinaigrette over the salad and toss to combine.
4. Serve the Nicoise Salad with Lemon Basil Vinaigrette immediately.

Nutrition Information:
Per serving: Calories 216, Net Carbs 3g, Total Fat 16g, Protein 12g

37. Nicoise Salad with Avocado and Bacon

Nicoise Salad with Avocado and Bacon is a unique take on the classic French salad. It is a healthy, light meal packed with flavor, featuring avocado, bacon, tomatoes, onion, and greens.

Serves 4 people. | Preparation Time 10 minutes. Ready time in 10 minutes.

Ingredients:
- 4 slices bacon
- 2 avocados, pitted and chopped
- 1 tomato, diced
- 1/2 onion, diced
- 4 cups of fresh greens
- 4 tablespoons olive oil
- 2 tablespoons freshly squeezed lemon juice
- Salt and pepper to taste

Instructions:
1. Heat a large skillet over medium heat and cook the bacon until crispy. Transfer to a plate lined with paper towels and allow to cool.
2. In a large bowl, combine the avocados, tomato, onion, and greens.

3. In a small bowl, combine the olive oil, lemon juice, salt, and pepper. Whisk until fully combined.

4. Drizzle the dressing over the salad and toss to coat.

5. Crumble the bacon over the top of the salad and serve.

Nutrition Information:

Calories: 282 kcal, Carbohydrates: 10 g, Protein: 7 g, Fat: 25 g, Saturated Fat: 4 g, Cholesterol: 16 mg, Sodium: 213 mg, Potassium: 540 mg, Fiber: 6 g, Sugar: 2 g, Vitamin A: 488 IU, Vitamin C: 13 mg, Calcium: 35 mg, Iron: 1 mg.

38. Nicoise Salad with Dried Cranberries

Nicoise Salad with Dried Cranberries is a fresh and flavorful dish that adds color and texture to any meal. Served chilled, this salad combines the classic flavors of a traditional Niçoise salad, with the sweetness of dried cranberries to create a delicious and healthy dish.

Serves: 4. | Preparation Time: 15 minutes. | Ready Time: 15 minutes.

Ingredients:
- 4 cups mixed greens
- 1/3 cup tomato slices
- 1/2 cup sliced cucumbers
- 2 boiled eggs, quartered
- 1/3 cup black olives
- 2 tablespoons olive oil
- 1 tablespoon lemon juice
- 1/4 teaspoon garlic powder
- 1/2 cup dried cranberries

Instructions:
1. In a large bowl, mix together the mixed greens, tomato slices, cucumbers, eggs and black olives.

2. In a small bowl, mix together the olive oil, lemon juice and garlic powder. Pour the dressing over the salad and toss to combine.

3. Sprinkle the dried cranberries over top. Serve chilled.

Nutrition Information (per serving):
270 calories, 20g fat, 11g carbohydrates, 4g protein.

39. Nicoise Salad with Artichoke Hearts and Olives

Tastes of the French Riviera come alive in this delicious Nicoise Salad with Artichoke Hearts and Olives. Perfect for an elegant lunch, it takes only minutes to prepare and is full of protein, vitamins and minerals.

Serving: 4 | Preparation Time: 15 minutes | Ready Time: 15 minutes

Ingredients:
- 2 hard boiled eggs, sliced
- 2 tablespoons olive oil
- 2 tablespoons red wine vinegar
- 1/2 teaspoon Dijon mustard
- 1 large head romaine lettuce, chopped
- 3 tablespoons capers
- 1/2 cup black olives, chopped
- 2 artichoke hearts, sliced
- 1/4 cup chopped fresh parsley

Instructions:
1. Whisk together the olive oil, red wine vinegar and Dijon mustard in a medium bowl, stirring until the dressing is evenly blended.
2. In a large bowl, combine the lettuce, capers, olives, artichoke hearts, parsley and eggs.
3. Pour the dressing over the salad and gently toss to combine.

Nutrition Information (per serving):
Calories: 192, Fat: 11 g, Carbohydrates: 8 g, Protein: 9 g, Sodium: 656 mg, Fiber: 4 g.

40. Nicoise Salad with Fennel and Dill

Nicoise Salad with Fennel and Dill is a delicious combination of fresh vegetables, crunchy legumes, and flavorful herbs. The perfect combination of sweet and savory flavors, this salad is ideal as a light but filling lunch or an impressive side dish.

Serving: 4-6 | Preparation Time: 15 minutes | Ready Time: 15 minutes

Ingredients:
* 2-3 cups arugula
* 2-3 cups dandelion greens
* 2 large tomatoes, diced
* 2 can of tuna, drained
* 2 cups cooked white beans
* 1/2 cup kalamata olives, pitted and halved
* 1 bulb fennel, thinly sliced
* 2 garlic cloves, minced
* 2 tbsp capers
* 2 tbsp apple cider vinegar
* 2-3 tbsp dill, chopped
* 2-3 tbsp fennel fronds, chopped
* Salt and pepper to taste

Instructions:
1. In a large bowl, toss together the arugula, dandelion greens, diced tomatoes, tuna, white beans, olives, fennel, garlic, capers, apple cider vinegar and herbs.
2. Season with salt and pepper to taste.
3. Serve chilled, or at room temperature.

Nutrition Information:
Calories: 392,
Carbs: 34g,
Fat: 8g,
Protein: 26g

41. Nicoise Salad with Pomegranate Seeds

This Nicoise Salad with Pomegranate Seeds is a delicious and nutritious meal full of Mediterranean flavors. It is chock-full of colorful vegetables paired with seared tuna and a simple yet flavorful vinaigrette.

Serving: 2 | Preparation Time: 10 minutes | Ready Time: 10 minutes

Ingredients:
- 2 heads of endive, roughly chopped
- 1 head radicchio, roughly chopped
- 2 tablespoons olive oil
- 4 ounces yellowfin tuna
- Salt and pepper, to taste
- 4 ounces baby spinach
- 4 ounces cherry tomatoes, halved
- 2 hard boiled eggs, chopped
- 2 ounces pomegranate seeds
- 1 tablespoon freshly squeezed lemon juice
- 1 tablespoon white wine vinegar
- 2 tablespoons capers
- 1 tablespoon freshly chopped parsley

Instructions:
1. Heat a large skillet over medium-high heat. Add the olive oil and tuna, season with salt and pepper, and cook for 3 to 4 minutes, flipping occasionally.
2. In a large bowl, combine the endive, radicchio, spinach, and tomatoes.
3. Add the cooked tuna, chopped eggs, and pomegranate seeds to the bowl.
4. In a separate bowl, whisk together the lemon juice, vinegar, capers, and parsley.
5. Pour the dressing over the salad and gently mix to combine.

Nutrition Information:
Calories: 312 | Protein: 24g | Carbs: 10g | Fat: 20g | Fiber: 4g

42. Nicoise Salad with Orzo

Nicoise Salad with Orzo combines classic Nicoise salad ingredients like olives, tomatoes, eggs and anchovies with orzo for a delicious and hearty salad dish.

Serving: This salad is enough for 6-8 people. | Preparation Time: 10 minutes | Ready Time: 25 minutes

Ingredients:
- 8 cups of cooked orzo
- 3 cups chunky diced tomatoes
- 1 cup diced red onions
- 1 cup diced cucumbers
- 1 cup black olives, sliced
- 6 ounces julienne cut anchovies
- 2 cups green beans, cooked
- 6 boiled eggs, quartered
- 4 tablespoons red wine vinegar
- 4 tablespoons extra-virgin olive oil
- 1 teaspoon of Dijon mustard
- Salt and freshly ground black pepper

Instructions:
1. Cook the orzo according to package instructions, then cool in an ice water bath. Drain and set aside.
2. In a large bowl, mix together the cooked orzo and all the diced vegetables.
3. In a small bowl, whisk together the red wine vinegar, extra-virgin olive oil and Dijon mustard. Pour the dressing over the orzo and vegetables, and toss to combine.
4. Season the salad with salt and pepper to taste.
5. Arrange the boiled eggs, anchovies and olives on top.

Nutrition Information:
Per serving (1/8 of total): 250 calories, 10g fat, 31g carbs, 8g protein, 3g fiber, 225mg sodium.

43. Nicoise Salad with Crispy Shallots

Introducing Nicoise Salad with Crispy Shallots, a delicious meal full of flavor and crunch! This salad is easy to put together and can be prepared in under an hour. It's perfect for a light lunch or summery dinner side.

Serving: 4 | Preparation Time: 10 minutes | Ready Time: Under 1 hour

Ingredients:
- 4 Tbsp olive oil
- 2 cloves garlic, minced
- 2 large shallots, sliced
- 5 oz mixed greens
- 1 red pepper, diced
- 1/2 cup cherry tomatoes, halved
- 1/2 avocado, chopped
- 2 hard-boiled eggs, quartered
- 6-8 oz canned tuna, drained
- 1/2 cup kalamata olives, pitted
- 2 Tbsp capers
- 2 Tbsp white balsamic vinaigrette
- Salt and black pepper, to taste

Instructions:
1. Heat 2 tablespoons of oil in a small skillet over medium-high heat. Add the garlic and shallots and cook, stirring occasionally, until the shallots are nicely browned, 5-7 minutes. Season with salt and pepper and set aside.
2. In a large salad bowl, combine the mixed greens, red pepper, tomatoes, avocado, eggs, tuna, olives and capers.
3. Drizzle with the remaining 2 tablespoons of oil and the white balsamic vinaigrette. Season with salt and pepper, to taste.
4. Top the salad with the crispy shallots and serve immediately.

Nutrition Information (per serving):
Calories: 404
Fat: 24g
Carbs: 16g
Protein: 29g
Fiber: 5g

44. Nicoise Salad with Radicchio

This light yet flavorful Nicoise Salad with Radicchio is a delightful combination of greens, vegetables, and hard boiled eggs. It's perfect for a light summer meal or as a healthy side dish.

Serving: 4 Preparation Time: 15 minutes Ready Time: 15 minutes

Ingredients:
- 5 cups mixed greens
- 2 cups shredded radicchio
- 1 red bell pepper, cut into thin strips
- 6 large eggs
- 1/2 red onion, cut into thin rings
- 4 ounces feta cheese
- 2 tablespoons olive oil
- 1 teaspoon white wine vinegar
- Salt and freshly ground black pepper, to taste

Instructions:
1. In a small saucepan, bring enough water to a boil. Gently add the eggs and cook for 9 to 10 minutes.
2. Discard the boiling water and rinse the eggs under cold running water. Peel and halve the eggs.
3. In a large salad bowl, combine the mixed greens, radicchio, red bell pepper, red onion, Fet cheese, and eggs.
4. To make the dressing, whisk together the olive oil, white wine vinegar, and salt and pepper in a small bowl until combined. Season to taste.
5. Pour the dressing over the salad and toss to combine. Serve.

Nutrition Information:
 Calories: 200, Fat: 11 g, Carbohydrates: 8 g, Protein: 12 g, Fiber: 3 g, Sugar: 3 g, Sodium: 276 mg

45. Nicoise Salad with Paprika Roasted Potatoes

Nicoise Salad with Paprika Roasted Potatoes is a classic French dish that is full of wholesome and nutritious ingredients. It's perfect for an easy weeknight dinner or special luncheon. This recipe features roasted potatoes with a paleo-friendly Paprika seasoning, succulent and flavorful tomatoes and green beans, along with a delicately poached egg and a homemade vinaigrette dressing.

Serving: 4 | Preparation Time: 10 minutes, | Ready Time: 45 minutes

Ingredients:
- 4 medium Yukon Gold Potatoes
- 1 tablespoon Paprika
- 1 tablespoon olive oil
- 2 large tomatoes
- 1 pound trimmed and blanched fresh green beans
- 4 eggs
- 2 tablespoons white wine vinegar
- 2 tablespoons extra-virgin olive oil
- 2 tablespoons minced shallots
- 1/4 teaspoon Dijon mustard
- freshly chopped parsley, for serving

Instruction:
1. Preheat oven to 400F. Cut potatoes into 1 to 2 inch cubes and transfer to a roasting pan. Sprinkle with paprika and olive oil, making sure all of the potatoes are lightly coated. Roast for about 30 minutes, or until lightly golden and cooked through.
2. Meanwhile, cook the eggs in a small saucepan of boiling water for about 6 to 8 minutes, until cooked but still soft. Remove the eggs with a slotted spoon and set aside.
3. Whisk together the white wine vinegar, extra-virgin olive oil, shallots, and Dijon mustard.
4. To assemble the salad, arrange the tomatoes and green beans in a bowl. Top with the roasted potatoes and poached eggs. Drizzle the vinaigrette over the salad and top with freshly chopped parsley.

Nutrition Information:
Per serving: 352 calories, 19.8 g fat, 3.2 g saturated fat, 265 mg sodium, 28.7 g carbohydrates, 5.3 g fiber, 5.9 g sugar, 11.3 g protein.

46. Nicoise Salad with Chive Vinaigrette

Nicoise Salad with Chive Vinaigrette is an easy yet delicious French-inspired salad recipe. With simple ingredients like potatoes, eggs, tomatoes, lettuce, and a homemade chive vinaigrette, it's sure to be a hit.

Serving: 4 | Preparation Time: 20 minutes | Ready Time: 20 minutes

Ingredients:
- 2 potatoes, diced and boiled
- 2 eggs, hard-boiled and cut into wedges
- 1 cup cherry tomatoes, sliced
- 1 head of butter lettuce, torn into bite-sized pieces
- 2 tablespoons white wine vinegar
- 2 teaspoons Dijon mustard
- 2 tablespoons chives, minced
- 2 tablespoons olive oil
- Salt and pepper to taste

Instructions:
1. In a small bowl, whisk together the vinegar, mustard, chives, olive oil, and salt and pepper.
2. In a large bowl, toss together the potatoes, eggs, tomatoes, and lettuce.
3. Pour the vinaigrette over the salad, and toss until everything is evenly coated.
4. Serve the salad immediately.

Nutrition Information:
Per Serving:
Calories: 172
Total Fat: 9g
Saturated Fat: 2 g
Cholesterol: 93mg
Sodium: 482 mg
Carbohydrates: 16 g
Protein: 6g

47. Nicoise Salad with Marinated Mushrooms

Nicoise Salad with Marinated Mushrooms is a delicious and healthy vegan meal that can be enjoyed for lunch or dinner. This salad is loaded with fresh, colorful vegetables, and marinated mushrooms that give it an umami-rich flavor. It's also a great way to get your daily dose of essential vitamins and minerals.

Serving: 4 | Preparation Time: 15 minutes

Ingredients:
- 4 ounces of Marinated Mushrooms
- 2 cups of Baby Spinach
- 1/2 cup of thinly sliced sweet cherry tomatoes
- 1/2 cup of blanched green beans
- 1/3 cup of pitted and quartered olives
- 1/2 cup of cooked, cubed red potatoes
- 1/3 cup of Falafel balls
- 2 tablespoons of Fresh Parsley, finely chopped
- 2 tablespoons of Fresh Dill, finely chopped
- 2 tablespoons of Balsamic Vinegar
- 2 tablespoons of extra-virgin Olive Oil
- Salt and Pepper, to taste

Instructions:
1. Start by marinating the mushrooms. In a shallow dish combine the Balsamic Vinegar and extra-virgin Olive Oil and whisk together. Add the mushrooms and coat evenly, then cover and let sit while you prepare the remaining ingredients.
2. In a large bowl, combine the Baby Spinach, Cherry Tomatoes, Green Beans, Olives, and Red Potatoes and toss together until combined.
3. Heat a medium skillet over medium-high heat and add the Falafel balls. Cook for 3-4 minutes, stirring occasionally until the Falafel balls are golden and cooked through.
4. Add the Falafel balls to the large bowl and mix together. Add the Parsley and Dill, then season with Salt and Pepper to taste.
5. Add the Marinated Mushrooms to the large bowl and mix until combined.
6. Serve and enjoy!

Nutrition Information (per serving):
Calories: 181
Fat: 11.5g
Carbohydrates: 18.5g
Protein: 5.5g
Fiber: 4g

48. Nicoise Salad with Roasted Asparagus

Nicoise Salad with Roasted Asparagus is a delicious and healthy dish that blends the flavors of crisp and tender asparagus with a traditional Nicoise salad. Perfect for lunch or as a light dinner, this salad is both easy to prepare and nutritious.

Serving: 4 | Preparation Time: 20 minutes | Ready Time: 20 minutes

Ingredients:
- 2 bunches asparagus, washed and trimmed
- 2 tablespoons olive oil
- salt and pepper to taste
- 2 tablespoons fresh lemon juice
- 2 cups cooked cannellini beans
- 1/2 cup cherry tomatoes, halved
- 2 hard-boiled eggs, quartered
- 2 tablespoons capers
- 4 anchovy fillets
- 2 tablespoons roughly chopped fresh parsley
- 8-10 small black olives
- 8 ounces cooked tuna, roughly flaked

Instructions:
1. Preheat oven to 400 degrees F. Place asparagus on a baking sheet and drizzle with olive oil. Season with salt and pepper and roast in preheated oven for 10 minutes.
2. Meanwhile, in a large bowl, whisk together lemon juice, and 3 tablespoons of olive oil.
3. Add cannellini beans, tomatoes, eggs, capers, anchovies, parsley, olives, and tuna.

4. Gently fold in roasted asparagus.
5. Divide among four plates and serve.

Nutrition Information:
Calories: 237, Total Fat: 9g, Saturated Fat: 1g, Cholesterol: 60mg,
Sodium: 517mg, Carbohydrates: 17g, Fiber: 7g, Protein: 24g

49. Nicoise Salad with Toasted Almonds

Nicoise Salad with Toasted Almonds is a traditional French salad made
with boiled potatoes, green beans, tomatoes, hard-boiled eggs, and tuna
topped with a flavorful dressing and toasted almonds for an added
crunch. This classic salad is as tantalizing to the taste buds as it is to the
eye.

Serving: 4 | Preparation Time: 20 minutes | Ready Time: 20 minutes

Ingredients:
- 2 potatoes, sliced into 1/2 inch cubes
- 1 cup green beans, trimmed
- 5 cherry tomatoes, halved
- 2 hard-boiled eggs, peeled and quartered
- 4 ounces canned tuna, drained
- 2 tablespoons slivered almonds, toasted
- 2 tablespoons white wine vinegar
- 1 tablespoon Dijon mustard
- 1 tablespoon olive oil
- Salt and pepper to taste

Instructions:
1. Preheat the oven to 375F and spread the almonds on an even layer on
a baking sheet. Toast for 5-7 minutes or until lightly golden. Set aside.
2. In a large pot, add the potatoes and enough salted water to cover.
Bring to a boil and cook for 8-10 minutes or until fork tender.
3. Add the green beans to the pot, and cook for another 5 minutes.
Drain and let cool.
4. In a small bowl, whisk together the white wine vinegar, Dijon mustard,
olive oil, salt and pepper.

5. Place the potatoes, green beans, tomatoes, hard-boiled eggs, and tuna in a large bowl. Pour over the dressing and toss to combine.
6. Sprinkle the toasted almonds over the salad and serve.

Nutrition Information:
Per serving
Calories: 262
Fat: 11g
Carbohydrates: 24g
Protein: 15g

50. Nicoise Salad with Red Onions

Nicoise Salad with Red Onions is a French-inspired salad that is brimming with fresh vegetables and topped with a tangy lemon-olive oil dressing. This vibrant and flavorful dish is sure to put a smile on your face. Serve this salad as a side to grilled fish or as a light lunch.

Serving: 4 | Preparation Time: 15 minutes | Ready Time: 15 minutes

Ingredients:
- 2 tablespoons lemon juice
- 2 teaspoons Dijon mustard
- 4 tablespoons olive oil
- 2 heads of Romaine lettuce, chopped
- 1 cherry tomatoes, halved
- 1 red onion, thinly sliced
- 1 green bell pepper, chopped
- 1 can of tuna in water, drained
- 1/2 cup black olives
- Salt and pepper to taste

Instructions:
1. In a small bowl, whisk together the lemon juice, mustard, and olive oil and set aside.
2. In a large bowl, combine the lettuce, tomatoes, red onion, bell pepper, tuna, and olives.
3. Pour the dressing over the salad and toss to coat all the ingredients.

4. Season with salt and pepper to taste.

Nutrition Information:
Per Serving: Calories- 312; Fat- 24 g; Carbohydrate- 12 g; Fiber - 5 g;
Protein- 13 g; Sodium- 283 mg

51. Nicoise Salad with Balsamic Mustard Dressing

Nicoise Salad with Balsamic Mustard Dressing is perfect for a summer
meal. This light yet vibrant salad features delectable flavors of tuna, hard-
boiled eggs, potatoes, olives, and tomatoes, making it a hearty and
healthy meal. The Balsamic Mustard Dressing adds an extra kick of
flavor, making this salad a surefire hit.

Serving Size: 4 | Preparation Time: 15 minutes | Ready Time: 15
minutes

Ingredients:
- 2 5-ounce cans tuna in water, drained
- 2 hard-boiled eggs, quartered
- 2 small red potatoes, cooked, and diced
- 1/2 cup cherry tomatoes, halved
- 1/2 cup black olives, halved
- 2 tablespoons fresh parsley, minced
- 2 tablespoons olive oil
- 1 tablespoon balsamic vinegar
- 1 tablespoon Dijon mustard
- Salt and pepper, to taste

Instructions:
1. In a large bowl, combine tuna, eggs, potatoes, olives, tomatoes, and
parsley.
2. In a small bowl, whisk together olive oil, vinegar, and mustard. Pour
the dressing over the salad and mix until evenly coated.
3. Season with salt and pepper, to taste. Serve immediately.

Nutrition Information:
Calories: 302; Total Fat 16g; Saturated Fat 2.5g; Cholesterol 114mg; Sodium 519mg; Total Carbohydrates 15.3g; Dietary Fiber 3.3g; Protein 21.3g; Vitamin A 3%; Vitamin C 22%; Calcium 4%; Iron 11%

52. Nicoise Salad with Roasted Red Bell Peppers

Nicoise Salad with Roasted Red Bell Peppers is a delicious fusion of French and Italian flavors. This vibrant dish is healthy, flavorful, and easy to put together. It can be served as a side or main dish and is perfect for lunch on a warm sunny day.

Serving: 4 | Preparation Time: 15 minutes | Ready Time: 30 minutes

Ingredients:
- 2 red bell peppers, cubed
- 2 tablespoons olive oil
- 1/2 pound small potatoes, boiled and halved
- 1 (5-ounce) can tuna in water, drained
- 1/4 cup kalamata olives
- 1/4 cup capers
- 2 tablespoons red wine vinegar
- 1 tablespoon Dijon mustard
- 2 tablespoons chopped fresh basil
- Salt and freshly ground black pepper to taste

Instructions:
1. Preheat the oven to 375F. Place the cubed bell peppers on a baking sheet and drizzle with the olive oil. Roast for 15 minutes or until softened and lightly browned. Set aside to cool.
2. In a large bowl, combine the roasted bell peppers, potatoes, tuna, olives, capers, red wine vinegar, Dijon mustard, and chopped fresh basil.
3. Season with salt and freshly ground black pepper, to taste.
4. Toss the salad lightly to combine all of the ingredients and serve.

Nutrition Information:
Serving size: 1/2 cup
Calories: 122 calories
Total Fat: 6 g
Saturated Fat: 1 g
Cholesterol: 13 mg
Sodium: 592 mg
Carbohydrates: 12 g
Fiber: 3 g
Protein: 6 g

53. Nicoise Salad with Fresh Basil

Nicoise Salad with Fresh Basil is a vibrant and flavorful salad, perfect for lunch or as a side dish. It is made with a colorful assortment of vegetables and comes together in about 30 minutes. This salad is full of vitamins, minerals, and healthy fats, making it a nutritious choice for any meal.

Serving: 4-6 | Preparation Time: 10 minutes | Ready Time: 30 minutes

Ingredients:
- 2 large potatoes, boiled, peeled, and cubed
- 2 cups cooked green beans
- 2 cups cherry tomatoes, halved
- 1/2 cup black olives, pitted
- 2 tablespoons capers
- 4 eggs, hard-boiled, peeled, and sliced
- 4 anchovies, chopped
- 1/2 cup fresh basil, torn into small pieces
- 2 tablespoons olive oil
- 1 tablespoon fresh lemon juice
- Salt and pepper, to taste

Instructions:
1. In a large bowl, combine the potatoes, green beans, tomatoes, olives, capers, eggs, and anchovies.

2. In a small bowl, whisk together the olive oil, lemon juice, salt and pepper. Pour the dressing over the salad and gently toss to combine.
3. Add the fresh basil and gently toss again. Serve immediately.

Nutrition Information:
Per Serving: 117 calories; 7.7 g fat; 5.2 g carbohydrates; 6.2 g protein; 86 mg cholesterol; 401 mg sodium.

54. Nicoise Salad with Anchovy Vinaigrette

Nicoise Salad with Anchovy Vinaigrette is a fresh and flavorful Mediterranean inspired salad filled with hard boiled eggs, olives, potatoes, green beans and tuna, all mixed together in a delicious and tangy anchovy vinaigrette.

Serving: 4 | Preparation Time: 30 minutes | Ready Time: 30 minutes

Ingredients:
- 4 eggs
- 1/2 cup Kalamata olives
- 1/2 cup boiled new potatoes
- 1/2 cup cooked green beans
- 1/2 can tuna
- 3 tablespoons anchovy paste
- 6 tablespoons olive oil
- 2 tablespoons white wine vinegar
- 2 tablespoons lemon juice
- 2 tablespoons chopped fresh parsley
- 2 tablespoons chopped fresh chives
- 2 tablespoons Dijon mustard
- 1/4 teaspoon sea salt
- 1/4 teaspoon freshly ground black pepper

Instructions:
1. Place eggs in a saucepan, cover with cold water and bring to a boil. Boil for 12 minutes, then remove from heat and soak in cold water for 5 minutes. Peel and then set aside in a large bowl.
2. Add the olives, potatoes and green beans to the eggs and set aside.

3. In a small bowl, whisk together the anchovy paste, olive oil, vinegar, lemon juice, parsley, chives, mustard, salt and pepper until well combined.
4. Pour the anchovy vinaigrette over the salad ingredients and mix until everything is evenly coated.
5. Divide the salad among four plates and top with canned tuna. Serve immediately.

Nutrition Information:
 Per Serving: Calories: 305, Total Fat: 22 g, Saturated Fat: 3 g, Cholesterol: 166 mg, Sodium: 410 mg, Carbohydrates: 15 g, Fiber: 2 g, Sugar: 1 g, Protein: 13 g.

55. Nicoise Salad with Oven Roasted Tomatoes

This flavorful Nicoise Salad with Oven Roasted Tomatoes is a delicious and nutritious meal. A combination of healthy vegetables, canned tuna, and homemade oven roasted tomatoes is a great way to enjoy a wholesome, satisfying salad.

Serving: 6 | Preparation Time: 15 minutes | Ready Time: 30 minutes

Ingredients:
• 6 vine-ripened tomatoes, cut into 2-inch wedges
• 1/4 cup extra-virgin olive oil
• 1 teaspoon garlic powder
• Salt and black pepper to taste
• 2 cups haricot verts
• 12 ounces canned tuna, drained and flaked
• 2 tablespoons dijon mustard
• 1/4 cup capers, drained
• 1/3 cup black olives, pitted
• 2 hard-boiled eggs, sliced
• 2 cups cooked potatoes, diced
• 2 tablespoons lemon juice
• 2 tablespoons chopped fresh parsley

Instructions:
1. Preheat the oven to 425F.
2. Arrange the tomatoes on a baking sheet and pour the olive oil over them. Sprinkle with garlic powder, salt and black pepper and roast for 15 minutes, until tender.
3. Cook the haricot verts according to package directions.
4. In a large bowl, combine the tuna, mustard, capers, olives, eggs, potatoes, lemon juice, and parsley. Add the warm roasted tomatoes and haricot verts and gently toss to combine.
5. Serve the salad warm or chilled.

Nutrition Information:
Calories: 274; Fat: 15g; Sodium: 528mg; Total carbohydrates: 19.4g; Protein: 15.3g

56. Nicoise Salad with Cherry Tomatoes

Nicoise Salad with Cherry Tomatoes is a healthy and delicious dish that can be enjoyed for a light lunch or dinner. This salad is a great way to get your crunch on and be sure to get lots of veggies in your day.

Serving: 4 | Preparation Time: 10 minutes | Ready Time: 10 minutes

Ingredients:
- 6 cups romaine lettuce, chopped
- 1 can tuna, drained and flaked
- 1/4 cup chopped red onion
- 1 cup cherry tomatoes, halved
- 1/2 cup kalamata olives, pitted and halved
- 2 boiled eggs, peeled and quartered
- 1/4 cup extra-virgin olive oil
- 2 tablespoons red wine vinegar
- Salt and pepper to taste

Instructions:
1. In a large bowl, combine romaine lettuce, tuna, red onion, cherry tomatoes, olives and boiled eggs.

2. In a separate small bowl, whisk together the extra-virgin olive oil, red wine vinegar, salt and pepper.
3. Drizzle the vinaigrette over the salad, tossing lightly to coat.
4. Serve and enjoy!

Nutrition Information:
Calories: 281; Fat: 16.7g; Carbohydrate: 11.2g; Protein: 22.1g

57. Nicoise Salad with Fregola

Nicoise Salad with Fregola is a delicious and nutritious summertime dinner. It features fregola, a healthy grain similar to couscous, blended with a variety of fresh vegetables and topped with a savory lemon vinaigrette. This simple, yet flavorful dish is sure to please everyone at the dinner table.

Serving: 4 | Preparation Time: 20 minutes | Ready Time: 30 minutes

Ingredients:
- 1 1/2 cups Fregola
- 1 cup cherry tomatoes, halved
- 2 cups steamed green beans
- 1 can (14oz) tuna in olive oil, drained
- 1/2 cup Kalamata olives, pitted
- 2 tablespoons Capers, drained
- 1 Shallot, finely chopped
- 4 tablespoons Extra Virgin Olive Oil
- 2 tablespoons Lemon Juice
- Salt and pepper to taste

Instructions:
1. In a large pot, cook the fregola according to package instructions. Drain and set aside.
2. In a medium bowl, combine the cherry tomatoes, green beans, tuna, olives, capers, and shallot.
3. In a small bowl, whisk together the olive oil and lemon juice.
4. Add the fregola to the bowl with the vegetables and tuna and lightly mix together.

5. Pour the dressing over the salad and season with salt and pepper to taste.
6. Serve immediately.

Nutrition Information:
Per 1 cup serving: Calories: 242, Fat: 11g, Carbohydrates: 22g, Protein: 12g, Dietary Fibre: 4g, Sodium: 575mg.

58. Nicoise Salad with Farro

Nicoise Salad with Farro: An elevated twist on the classic French Nicoise Salad, this is a nutrient packed dish combining protein and fiber rich farro, fresh vegetables, and egg. Enjoy it on its own as a light lunch or serve it as a side.

Serving: 4 | Preparation Time: 10 minutes | Ready Time: 20 minutes

Ingredients:
- 2 cups farro, cooked according to package instructions
- 2 cups cherry tomatoes, halved
- 2 cups cucumber, sliced into 1-inch pieces
- 2 hard-boiled eggs, halved
- 8 ounces albacore tuna
- 2 tablespoons olive oil
- 2 tablespoons lemon juice
- 2 tablespoons white balsamic vinegar
- 2 teaspoons dijon mustard
- 2 teaspoons capers
- 2 tablespoons freshly chopped parsley
- Salt and pepper, to taste

Instructions:
1. In a large bowl, combine farro, tomatoes, cucumber, eggs, and tuna.
2. In a small bowl, whisk together olive oil, lemon juice, balsamic vinegar, dijon mustard, capers, and parsley.
3. Pour the dressing over the salad and stir to combine.
4. Season with salt and pepper, to taste.
5. Divide between four plates and enjoy.

Nutrition Information:
345 Calories, 19g Fat, 28g Carbs, 11g Protein

59. Nicoise Salad with Radish Sprouts

Nicoise Salad with Radish Sprouts is a delicious and healthy lunch or side option that is loaded with vibrant flavors. The combination of tuna, potatoes, and radish sprouts makes it super tasty and nutritious.

Serving: 4 | Preparation Time: 20 minutes | Ready Time: 20 minutes

Ingredients:
-2 tablespoons capers
-2 cans tuna in olive oil
-2 potatoes, boiled and diced
-2 Cups radish sprouts
-4 tablespoons olive oil
-4 tablespoons red wine vinegar
-1 teaspoon Dijon mustard
-Salt and pepper to taste

Instructions:
1. In a large bowl, mix together capers, tuna, potatoes, and radish sprouts.
2. In a small bowl, whisk together olive oil, red wine vinegar, and Dijon mustard.
3. Drizzle dressing over salad and season with salt and pepper to taste.
4. Serve chilled.

Nutrition Information:
Per serving, this dish contains approximately 250 calories,13g fat, 24g protein, 17g carbohydrates, and 4g fiber.

60. Nicoise Salad with Sesame Seeds

Nicoise Salad with Sesame Seeds is a healthy and delicious salad for a light lunch or side dish. It has a delightful combination of crunchy and savory elements that make it a standout in any meal. Serving 8, this preparation is quick and easy and ready in 10 minutes.

Serving: 8 | Preparation Time: 5 minutes | Ready Time: 10 minutes

Ingredients:
- 6 cups mixed greens
- 2 tablespoons olive oil
- 2 tablespoons freshly squeezed lemon juice
- 2 tablespoons sesame seeds
- 2 (15-ounce) cans tuna, drained
- 2 hard boiled eggs, sliced
- 2 Roma tomatoes, cored and diced
- 6 black olives, pitted and halved
- 2 tablespoons diced red onion
- Salt and pepper, to taste

Instructions:
1. In a large bowl, gently toss together mixed greens, olive oil, lemon juice, and sesame seeds.
2. Add tuna, eggs, tomatoes, olives, and red onion, and mix until all of the ingredients are evenly blended.
3. Season with salt and pepper, to taste.
4. Serve immediately.

Nutrition Information (per serving):
Calories: 158; Fat: 6.5g; Carbohydrates: 9.2g; Protein: 14.5g; Cholesterol: 53.5mg; Sodium: 241.6mg; Fiber: 1.7g

61. Nicoise Salad with Wasabi Peas

Nicoise Salad with Wasabi Peas is a flavorful combination of salty, sweet and tangy ingredients blended together for an irresistible dish. The combination of salty tuna and sweet yellow peppers, vibrant green beans, creamy boiled eggs and crunchy wasabi peas adds flavor and texture to the salad. This healthy salad is surprisingly light and nutrient-packed, and ready in minutes!

Serving: 4-5 | Preparation Time: 10 minutes | Ready Time: 10 minutes

Ingredients:
- 2 cans Tuna, drained
- 2 cups Green Beans, boiled
- 2 boiled Eggs, shelled
- 2 Red Peppers, thinly sliced
- 2 Yellow Peppers, thinly sliced
- 1/2 cup Wasabi Peas
- 2 tablespoons Olive Oil
- 2 tablespoons Red Wine Vinegar
- 1 teaspoon Mustard
- Salt and Pepper, to taste

Instructions:
1. In a large bowl, combine the tuna, green beans, eggs, peppers and wasabi peas.
2. In a smaller bowl, mix together the olive oil, red wine vinegar, mustard, salt and pepper.
3. Pour the dressing over the salad and toss to combine.
4. Serve immediately or chill for 2-3 hours for best flavor.

Nutrition Information:
Calories: 255
Fat: 12.2g
Carbohydrates: 15.1g
Protein: 18.9g

62. Nicoise Salad with Sauteed Prawns

Nicoise Salad with Sauteed Prawns is a classic Mediterranean salad bursting with flavor and texture. It makes a full meal with the addition of sautéed prawns, and is perfectly balanced with a tangy vinaigrette dressing.

Serve 4-6. | Preparation Time: 15 minutes. | Ready Time: 25 minutes.

Ingredients:
- 20-25 large peeled and deveined prawns

65

- 2 tablespoons olive oil
- 3 tablespoons freshly squeezed lemon juice
- 1 teaspoon dried oregano
- 1 teaspoon garlic powder
- 1 pound of red potatoes, boiled and cubed
- 1 head of romaine lettuce, finely chopped
- 2 cups cooked green beans, cut into 1 inch pieces
- 1 avocado, peeled and cubed
- 1/2 cup sliced black olives
- 1 pint of cherry tomatoes, halved
- 4 hard boiled eggs, quartered
- 1 red onion, diced
- Salt and pepper to taste
- For the dressing:
- 3 tablespoons olive oil
- 2 tablespoons white wine vinegar
- 1 tablespoon Dijon mustard
- 1 teaspoon fresh garlic, minced
- 1 teaspoon dried oregano
- Salt and pepper to taste

Instructions:

1. Preheat the oven to 400F.
2. In a small bowl, combine the olive oil, lemon juice, oregano, garlic powder and some salt and pepper. Mix well until combined.
3. Place the prawns on a baking sheet lined with parchment paper. Pour the marinade over the prawns and use your hands to make sure each prawn is fully coated with the marinade.
4. Bake the prawns for 8-10 minutes or until they are cooked through.
5. Meanwhile, in a salad bowl, combine the potatoes, lettuce, green beans, avocado, olives, cherry tomatoes, and red onion.
6. Make the dressing by combining the olive oil, white wine vinegar, Dijon mustard, garlic, oregano, and salt and pepper in a medium-sized bowl. Whisk until combined.
7. To assemble the salad, pour the dressing over the salad ingredients and gently mix until everything is evenly coated. Place the prawns and eggs around the salad and season with additional salt and pepper if needed.

Nutrition Information:
 Calories 557, Total Fat 26g, Saturated Fat 3.5g, Cholesterol 310mg,
Total Carbohydrates 36g, Dietary Fiber 7g, Sugars 6g, Protein 37g

63. Nicoise Salad with Pickled Onions

Nicoise Salad with Pickled Onions is a fresh, hearty and flavorful salad
that is sure to please. This delightful salad combines the crunch of oven-
roasted potatoes, hard-boiled eggs, and fresh green beans with a flavorful
olive vinaigrette, anchovies, and pickled onions. It is a fantastic side dish
for dinner or a light lunch.

Serving: 6 | Preparation Time: 20 minutes | Ready Time: 60 minutes

Ingredients:
-3 large potatoes, roasted
-1 1/2 cups green beans, steamed
-3 hard-boiled eggs, quartered
-1 cup olives (black or green)
-1 can anchovies, drained
-Pickled onions, to taste
-Olive oil vinaigrette, to taste

Instructions:
1. Preheat your oven to 400 degrees F.
2. Slice the potatoes into wedges, spread on a baking tin, and roast in the
oven for 20 minutes.
3. While the potatoes are roasting, bring a pot of lightly salted water to
boil over high heat. Add the green beans and boil for five minutes until
tender.
4. Place eggs in a small saucepan with cold water and bring to the boil.
Boil for 8 minutes for a hard-boiled egg.
5. In a large bowl, assemble the potatoes, green beans, eggs, olives,
anchovies, and pickled onions.
6. Drizzle your desired amount of olive oil vinaigrette and toss
everything together until evenly mixed.
7. Serve and enjoy.

Nutrition Information:
Per serving of Nicoise Salad with Pickled Onions:
Calories: 319, Total Fat: 16 g, Cholesterol: 12 mg, Sodium: 878 mg, Total Carbohydrate: 39 g, Fiber: 6 g, Sugar: 4 g, Protein: 10 g.

64. Nicoise Salad with Mango

This Nicoise Salad with Mango is the perfect light summer salad, with an exciting blend of flavors. It is filled with fresh ingredients, including tomatoes, eggs, and mango, and is served with a tangy balsamic vinaigrette.

Serving: 8 | Preparation Time: 15 minutes | Ready Time: 15 minutes

Ingredients:
- 2 tablespoons extra-virgin olive oil
- 2 tablespoons balsamic vinegar
- 2 tablespoons honey
- Salt and freshly ground black pepper
- 1 head romaine lettuce, cut into thin strips
- 1 red tomato, diced
- 2 hard boiled eggs, quartered
- 1 avocado, cut into slices
- 1 mango, peeled and cubed

Instructions:
1. In a small bowl, whisk together the olive oil, balsamic vinegar, and honey. Season with salt and pepper to taste.
2. In a large salad bowl, combine the lettuce, tomato, eggs, avocado, and mango.
3. Pour the dressing over the salad and toss until everything is evenly coated.
4. Serve immediately.

Nutrition Information:
Calories: 107; Fat: 7.4g; Carbohydrates: 10.2g; Protein: 3.1g; Sodium: 35mg; Fiber: 1.9g; Sugar: 6.8g.

65. Nicoise Salad with Roasted Parsnips

Nicoise Salad with Roasted Parsnips is a delicious dish that combines vibrant flavors of lemon and herbs with roasted root vegetables. The perfect combination of seasonal produce and lighter proteins, this hearty salad can be enjoyed anytime of year.

Serving: 4 | Preparation Time: 15 minutes | Ready Time: 45 minutes

Ingredients:
-2 large parsnips, cut into cubes
-2 tablespoons olive oil
-2 tablespoons fresh lemon juice
-2 tablespoons chopped fresh parsley
-1 cup cherry tomatoes, halved
-1/4 cup kalamata olives
-1/4 cup cooked green beans
-4 hard-boiled eggs, quartered
-2 tablespoons capers
-1/4 cup crumbled feta cheese
-Salt and pepper, to taste

Instructions:
1. Preheat the oven to 400 degrees Fahrenheit.
2. Place the parsnip cubes on one side of a baking sheet and drizzle with the olive oil. Roast for 20 to 25 minutes, or until golden and tender.
3. In a large bowl, whisk together the lemon juice and parsley until combined.
4. To the bowl, add the roasted parsnips, tomatoes, olives, green beans, eggs, capers and feta cheese. Mix until everything is combined and evenly coated with the lemon dressing.
5. Season the salad with salt and pepper, to your liking.
6. Serve the Nicoise salad and enjoy!

Nutrition Information:
Per serving, this salad contains 325 calories, 20.1 g fat, 13.8 g protein, and 24.5 g carbohydrates.

66. Nicoise Salad with Black Olives

Nicoise Salad with Black Olives is a delicious and easy to prepare meal that is not only healthy but also full of flavor.

Serves 4; | Preparation Time 10 minutes; Ready in 20 minutes.

Ingredients:
- 4 cups cherry tomatoes
- 2 cans of tuna, drained
- 2 potatoes, boiled
- 1/2 cup black olives
- 2 cloves garlic, minced
- 1/4 cup extra-virgin olive oil
- Juice of 1 lemon
- 2 tablespoons freshly chopped parsley
- Salt and freshly ground pepper to taste

Instructions:
1. In a bowl, combine tomatoes, tuna, potatoes, olives, garlic, olive oil, lemon juice, parsley, salt and pepper.
2. Mix everything together thoroughly.
3. Serve the salad in individual plates or a salad bowl.

Nutrition Information (per serving):
Calories: 247, Fat: 10.5 g, Carbohydrates: 22.3 g, Protein: 15.5 g, Fiber: 3.6 g

67. Nicoise Salad with Macadamia Nuts

This simple yet delicious Nicoise Salad is the perfect lunch or light dinner. Topped with roasted macadamia nuts, it offers a delightful mixture of flavors and textures.

Serving: 4 | Preparation Time: 10 minutes | Ready Time: 25 minutes

Ingredients:
-3/4 cup cooked green beans

-2 cups cherry tomatoes, halved
-1/2 cup cooked baby potatoes
-1/4 cup red onion, sliced
-1/2 cup cooked or canned tuna
-1/2 cup pitted kalamata olives
-1/2 cup roasted macadamia nuts
-2 tablespoons of red wine vinegar
-4 tablespoons of olive oil
-Salt and pepper, to taste

Instructions:
1. Preheat oven to 400F.
2. Place macadamia nuts on a baking sheet and roast for 5 minutes.
3. In a large bowl, combine green beans, cherry tomatoes, baby potatoes, red onion, tuna, and kalamata olives.
4. In a small bowl, whisk together red wine vinegar, olive oil, salt and pepper.
5. Pour dressing over salad and toss to combine.
6. Top with roasted macadamia nuts and serve.

Nutrition Information:
Calories: 340; Protein: 14g; Fat: 24g; Carbohydrates: 14g; Fiber: 2g; Sugar: 3g; Sodium: 440mg

68. Nicoise Salad with Soft Boiled Egg

Nicoise Salad with Soft-Boiled Egg is a delicious and healthy way to get a meal in one bowl. Rich in omega-3s and other beneficial fatty acids, this salad is sure to leave your taste buds, and your stomach, satisfied.

Serving: 4 | Preparation Time: 15 minutes | Ready Time: 30 minutes

Ingredients:
- 1/2 cup of cooked baby potatoes, quartered
- 1/2 cup cooked green beans
- 4 hard boiled eggs
- 1 sweet red pepper, cut into strips
- 2 cans tuna chunks in brine

- 1 teaspoon of Dijon mustard
- 2 teaspoons of olive oil
- Salt and pepper
- 2 tablespoons capers
- 2 tablespoons of chopped olives
- 2 tablespoons of lemon juice

Instructions:
1. Boil the potatoes for about 10 minutes, until fork tender. Drain and set aside.
2. Boil the eggs in a separate pot for about 5 minutes. Let cool before peeling and setting aside.
3. Heat the 2 teaspoons of oil in a skillet on medium heat. Add the green beans and red pepper, and season with salt and pepper. Cook until the vegetables are crisp and tender.
4. Drain the tuna and add to the skillet. Heat for 1-2 minutes, then add the mustard. Stir to combine.
5. In a large bowl, assemble the salad. Layer the potatoes, green beans, red pepper, eggs, tuna, capers, olives, and a drizzle of lemon juice.
6. Serve and enjoy!

Nutrition Information:
Calories: 343 Calories;
Total Fat: 12g;
Saturated Fat: 2g;
Cholesterol: 191mg;
Sodium: 538mg;
Total Carbohydrate: 19g;
Dietary Fiber: 5.4g;
Protein: 35.4g.

69. Nicoise Salad with Camembert Cheese

Nicoise Salad with Camembert Cheese is a unique and highly flavorful dish that combines fresh vegetables, flavorful greens, and creamy Camembert cheese. This gorgeous salad is perfect for serving at upscale dinner parties or as a light lunch on a hot afternoon.

Serving: 4 | Preparation Time: 15 minutes | Ready Time: 15 minutes

Ingredients:
- 8 ounces mixed salad greens
- 1/2 cup pre-cut green beans
- 2 radishes, sliced
- 2 tablespoons vinaigrette
- 4 ounces Camembert cheese, cubed
- 1 tablespoon chopped fresh parsley

Instructions:
1. Place the salad greens on four dinner plates.
2. In a medium bowl, toss the green beans, radishes, and vinaigrette together.
3. Divide the green bean mixture among the dinner plates, and top each salads with cubes of Camembert cheese.
4. Garnish each salad with chopped parsley.

Nutrition Information:
Serving Size: 1
Calories: 103
Total Fat: 7.8g
Total Carbohydrates: 1.6g
Protein: 5.6g

70. Nicoise Salad with Mustard Vinaigrette

Nicoise Salad with Mustard Vinaigrette is a classic French-inspired salad dish with a fresh and light yet deeply flavorful and satisfying flavor profile. It is an ideal summertime side or main dish, with a balanced combination of greens, vegetables, and protein, all combined with an intensely flavorful mustard vinaigrette.

Serves 4. Prep time: 20 minutes. | Ready Time: 20 minutes.

Ingredients:
- 6-8 cups romaine and/or mixed greens
- 1/2 cup cherry tomatoes, halved

- 1 small red onion, diced
- 1/3 cup pitted Kalamata olives, halved
- 1 15-ounce can of cannellini beans, drained and rinsed
- 1/2 cup cooked, diced potatoes
- 1/4 cup feta cheese, crumbled
- 4 hard boiled eggs, quartered
- 2 tablespoons Dijon mustard
- 2 tablespoons red wine vinegar
- 2 teaspoons honey
- 2 tablespoons olive oil
- salt and pepper to taste

Instructions:
1. In a large bowl, combine romaine and/or mixed greens, cherry tomatoes, red onion, Kalamata olives, and cannellini beans.
2. In a separate bowl, whisk together the Dijon mustard, red wine vinegar, honey, and olive oil.
3. Pour the mustard and vinegar dressing over the salad and season to taste with salt and pepper.
4. Toss the salad to combine and serve immediately, topped with feta cheese, potatoes, and eggs.

Nutrition Information (per serving):
350 calories; 15 g fat; 940 mg sodium; 33 g carbohydrate; 6 g fiber; 14 g protein.

71. Nicoise Salad with White Beans

Nicoise Salad with White Beans is a delicious, healthy, and easy to make salad perfect for summertime meals. This salad is packed with fresh flavors such as tuna, potatoes, tomatoes, and olives, plus lots of protein from white beans. It's a great way to make a meal out of a salad.

Serving: 4 | Preparation Time: 15 minutes | Ready Time: 15 minutes

Ingredients:
- 4 cups chopped romaine lettuce
- 4 ounces tuna canned in olive oil

- 4-5 boiled red potatoes (cut in half)
- 2 cups cooked white beans
- 10 cherry tomatoes (halved)
- 2 tablespoons capers
- 1/4 cup pitted kalamata olives
- 2 tablespoons fresh chopped parsley
- 1 tablespoon fresh chopped dill
- 2 tablespoons olive oil
- 2 tablespoons fresh lemon juice
- 1-2 tablespoons dijon mustard
- Salt and pepper to taste

Instructions:
1. In a large bowl combine the lettuce, tuna, potatoes, white beans, cherry tomatoes, capers, olives, and herbs in a single layer.
2. In a small bowl whisk together the olive oil, lemon juice, mustard, salt, and pepper.
3. Pour the dressing over the salad and gently mix until everything is coated.
4. Serve the salad at room temperature.

Nutrition Information:
Calories: 226
Fat: 9g
Carbohydrates: 24g
Protein: 14g
Cholesterol: 16mg
Sodium: 270mg
Fiber: 7g

72. Nicoise Salad with Grilled Halloumi

Nicoise Salad with Grilled Halloumi: A vibrant, light, yet filling salad made with fresh, summery ingredients, this Nicoise salad with grilled Halloumi is sure to be a hit with family and friends.

Serving: 4 | Preparation Time: 15 minutes | Ready Time: 15 minutes

Ingredients:
- 200g halloumi, sliced
- 2 tbsp olive oil
- A bunch of fresh basil leaves
- 2 hard-boiled eggs, quartered
- 2 handfulls of cherry tomatoes
- Half a cucumber, sliced
- A handful of kalamata olives
- 2 tbsp capers
- 4 anchovy fillets
- 2 cups of lettuce leaves
- 2 tbsp red wine vinegar
- Salt and pepper, to taste

Instructions:
1. Heat some olive oil in a grill pan over a medium heat and cook the halloumi until golden brown.
2. Once cooked, remove the halloumi from the pan and set aside.
3. In a large bowl, combine the lettuce leaves, tomatoes, cucumber, olives, capers, anchovies, basil leaves and hard-boiled eggs.
4. Drizzle the red wine vinegar over the salad and season with salt and pepper, to taste.
5. Add the halloumi and toss everything together.
6. Serve the Nicoise salad on individual plates and enjoy.

Nutrition Information:
Each serving provides approximately 200 calories, 12g fat, 14g carbohydrates, and 10g protein.

73. Nicoise Salad with Spring Onion

Nicoise Salad with Spring Onion is a fresh and flavorful salad that is a great addition to any meal. It is full of nutritious ingredients such as tuna, green beans, olives, tomatoes, potatoes, hard-boiled eggs, anchovies, onions, and vinaigrette.

Serves: 4 | Preparation Time: 20 minutes | Ready Time: 20 minutes

Ingredients:
-1 (5-oz) can chunk light tuna in water
-1/2 cup sliced Spring Onion
-1/2 cup cooked green beans
-1/4 cup small black olives
-1/2 cup cherry tomatoes, halved
-6 small boiled potatoes, quartered
-2 hard-boiled eggs, cut into wedges
-4 anchovy fillets
-4 tablespoons vinaigrette

Instructions:
1. Drain the tuna and place it in a large bowl.
2. Add the Spring Onion, green beans, olives, tomatoes, potatoes and eggs.
3. Add the anchovy fillets and vinaigrette and gently stir to combine.
4. Divide the salad among four serving plates.

Nutrition Information:
Calories: 353, Protein: 28 g, Fat: 15 g, Carbohydrate: 25 g, Sodium: 488.6 mg, Fiber: 4.5 g

74. Nicoise Salad with Paprika Tuna

Nicoise Salad with Paprika Tuna is a delicious and nutritious summer meal, perfect for lunch or dinner. It includes a mix of garden-fresh lettuce, tomatoes, hardboiled eggs, olives and paprika flavored tuna, served with a light vinaigrette dressing. This dish is an excellent source of lean protein, fiber and vitamins.
Serving: 4 | Preparation Time: 10 minutes | Ready Time: 15 minutes

Ingredients:
- 2 tomatoes, diced
- 6 cups lettuce of choice, chopped
- 2 hard boiled eggs, quartered
- 2 cans paprika flavored tuna, drained
- 1/2 cup black olives
- 1/3 cup olive oil

- 2 tablespoons red wine vinegar
- 1/2 teaspoon minced garlic
- 1/2 teaspoon dijon mustard
- salt and pepper, to taste

Instructions:
1. In a small bowl, whisk together the olive oil, red wine vinegar, garlic, dijon mustard, salt and pepper.
2. In a large bowl, combine lettuce, tomatoes, eggs and tuna.
3. Drizzle the vinaigrette over the salad and toss to coat.
4. Taste and adjust seasoning as necessary.
5. Garnish with black olives and serve.

Nutrition Information:
Per serving: 396 calories, 27g fat, 14g carbohydrates, 23g protein.

75. Nicoise Salad with Pickled Red Cabbage

Nicoise Salad with Pickled Red Cabbage is a delicious and healthy combination of cooked fresh vegetables and pickled red cabbage. This brightly colored salad is light, flavorful, and perfect for a summer meal.

Serving: 4 | Preparation Time: 15 minutes | Ready Time: 15 minutes

Ingredients:
• 5-6 cups cooked fresh vegetables, such as green beans, tomatoes, bell peppers, asparagus, and potatoes
• 1/4 cup olive oil
• 2 tablespoons red wine vinegar
• 2 tablespoons Dijon mustard
• 1/2 teaspoon salt
• 1/2 teaspoon freshly ground pepper
• 1 cup pickled red cabbage, thinly sliced
• 1/4 cup finely chopped fresh herbs, such as basil, parsley, and chive

Instructions:
1. In a large bowl, combine the cooked vegetables, olive oil, vinegar, mustard, salt, and pepper. Toss well to combine.

2. Add in the pickled red cabbage and fresh herbs and toss gently to combine.
3. Divide the Nicoise salad among 4 serving plates. Enjoy immediately.

Nutrition Information (per serving):
Calories: 181, Fat: 13g, Cholesterol: 0mg, Sodium: 573mg, Carbohydrates: 15g, Protein: 4g, Fiber: 3g.

76. Nicoise Salad with Edamame Hummus

This Nicoise Salad with Edamame Hummus is a healthy and flavorful meal packed with nutritious vegetables. It's colorful and sure to be a crowd-pleaser!

Serving: 4 | Preparation Time: 15 minutes | Ready Time: 15 minutes

Ingredients:
- 2 heads of romaine or butter lettuce
- 2 hard boiled eggs, sliced
- 2 tomatoes, diced
- 1/4 cup kalamata olives
- 1/4 cup edamame hummus, store bought or homemade
- 2 tablespoons olive oil
- Freshly ground black pepper, to taste
- 2 tablespoons white balsamic vinegar

Instructions:
1. Wash and dry the lettuce and rip into bite size pieces. Place in a large bowl.
2. Add the tomatoes, eggs, and olives.
3. In a small bowl, combine the edamame hummus, olive oil, black pepper and white balsamic vinegar and whisk until everything is evenly combined.
4. Pour the hummus dressing over the salad and toss everything together until evenly coated.

Nutrition Information (per serving):
Calories: 232 kcal, Fat: 16g, Carbohydrates: 9g, Protein: 12g, Fiber: 2g,
Sodium: 354mg

77. Nicoise Salad with Curried Chickpeas

Nicoise Salad with Curried Chickpeas is a delicious and healthful
Mediterranean-inspired meal that combines the flavors of kale,
chickpeas, bell peppers, and olives. The addition of a creamy curried
dressing makes this salad an incredibly flavorful dish.

Serving: 4 | Preparation Time: 15 minutes | Ready Time: 30 minutes

Ingredients:
- 2 tablespoons olive oil
- 2 teaspoons curry powder
- 1 can (15 ounces) chickpeas, drained and rinsed
- 4 cups kale, chopped
- 1 red bell pepper, diced
- 1/2 cup black olives, pitted and halved
- 1/4 cup red onion, finely diced
- 2 tablespoons fresh parsley, chopped
- 1/4 teaspoon sea salt
- 1/4 cup extra-virgin olive oil
- 2 tablespoons apple cider vinegar
- 1 tablespoon honey (optional)
- 2 tablespoons freshly squeezed lemon juice

Instructions:
1. Preheat oven to 375F.
2. In a medium bowl, mix together 2 tablespoons of olive oil and curry
powder.
3. Add in the chickpeas and mix together until evenly coated.
4. Spread chickpeas onto a baking sheet and bake for 25 minutes,
flipping once halfway through.
5. In a large bowl, combine kale, bell pepper, olives, red onion, parsley,
and sea salt.

6. In a small bowl, whisk together extra-virgin olive oil, apple cider vinegar, honey, and lemon juice.
7. Once chickpeas are done, add to the large bowl and mix together.
8. Pour dressing over salad and mix together. Serve warm or cold.

Nutrition Information:
Calories: 254 kcal, Carbohydrates: 16 g, Protein: 4 g, Fat: 20 g, Saturated Fat: 3 g, Sodium: 328 mg, Potassium: 286 mg, Fiber: 5 g, Sugar: 4 g, Vitamin A: 3120 IU, Vitamin C: 66 mg, Calcium: 86 mg, Iron: 2 mg.

78. Nicoise Salad with Saffron Aioli

Nicoise Salad with Saffron Aioli is an exquisite and flavorful dish for a luxurious lunch or dinner. The combination of fresh vegetables, tuna, and the fragrant aioli will have your taste buds delighted.

Serving: 4 | Preparation Time: 20 minutes | Ready Time: 40 minutes

Ingredients:
- 2 small cucumbers, cut into quarters
- 200g of cooked tuna, drained
- 2 large tomatoes, cut into wedges
- 200g of beans, canned, drained and rinsed
- 30g black olives
- 2 small red onions, cut into wedges
- 4 eggs, hard-boiled, peeled and quartered
- 4 tablespoons olive oil
- Salt and freshly-ground black pepper, to taste
For Saffron Aioli:
- 1 clove garlic, minced
- 1/2 teaspoon saffron threads
- 2 tablespoons lemon juice
- 2 egg yolks
- 1 cup extra-virgin olive oil

Instructions:
1. Preheat oven to 375°F (190°C).

2. Arrange cucumbers, tuna, tomatoes, beans, olives and red onions in a single layer in a large roasting pan. Drizzle with the olive oil and season with salt and black pepper.
3. Roast for 20 minutes, stir once or twice during cooking.
4. Meanwhile, make the Saffron Aioli. In a small bowl, combine the garlic, saffron, lemon juice and egg yolks. Using an immersion blender, gradually blend in the olive oil until the sauce is thick and creamy.
5. When the vegetables are ready, arrange them on a large plate. Add the eggs and spoon over the Saffron Aioli. Serve at once.

Nutrition Information:
Per Serving: 337 Calories; 23g Fat; 20g Protein; 16g Carbohydrate; 4g Dietary Fiber; 59mg Cholesterol; 562mg Sodium.

79. Nicoise Salad with Avocado and Figs

Nicoise Salad with Avocado and Figs is a French inspired dish that packs a flavorful punch. The combination of juicy figs, creamy avocado, and a classic French vinaigrette makes this spinach base salad an exceptional side dish to enjoy or an elegant centerpiece for a light lunch or dinner.

Serving: 4 | Preparation Time: 15 minutes | Ready Time: 15 minutes

Ingredients:
- 11/2 cups baby spinach
- 2 ripe avocados, cubed
- 5 ripe figs, cubed
- 4 hard boiled eggs, quartered
- 2 tablespoons white balsamic vinegar
- 2 tablespoons extra-virgin olive oil
- 1/2 teaspoon Dijon mustard
- Salt and pepper to taste

Instruction:
1. In a large bowl, mix together the baby spinach, cubed avocado, cubed figs, and quartered hard boiled eggs.
2. In a small bowl, combine the white balsamic vinegar, olive oil, and Dijon mustard. Season to taste with salt and pepper.

3. Drizzle the dressing over the salad and toss everything together.
4. Serve the Nicoise Salad with Avocado and Figs.

Nutrition Information (per serving):
Calories: 239, Protein: 8.2g, Fat: 17.2g, Carbs: 15.5g, Fiber: 5.9g, Sugars: 5.3g

80. Nicoise Salad with Pickled Fennel

Nicoise Salad with Pickled Fennel is a light and flavorful summer salad that can be prepared in minutes. This delicious salad combines the flavors of pickled fennel, boiled potatoes, tomatoes, and hard-boiled eggs with a zesty dressing for a healthy and satisfying meal.

Serving: 4 | Preparation Time: 15 minutes | Ready Time: 15 minutes

Ingredients:
- 2 tablespoons red wine vinegar
- 1 teaspoon Dijon mustard
- 1/4 cup olive oil
- 3 tablespoons chopped fresh basil
- 1 teaspoon sugar
- 1 tablespoon capers
- Kosher salt
- Freshly ground black pepper
- 2 small fennel bulbs, slightly trimmed and thinly sliced
- 1 cup cooked new potatoes, cut into cubes
- 2 firm-ripe tomatoes, cut into wedges
- 4 hard-boiled eggs, halved

Instructions:
1. In a medium bowl, whisk together the red wine vinegar, Dijon mustard, olive oil, basil, sugar, and capers. Season with salt and pepper, to taste.
2. In a large bowl, combine the fennel, potatoes, tomatoes, and egg. Pour the dressing over the salad and toss to combine.
3. Divide the Nicoise Salad among four plates and serve.

Nutrition Information:
Serving Size: 1/4 of recipe; Servings per person: 1; Calories: 446; Fat: 25.5g; Carbs: 40.5g; Protein: 13g

81. Nicoise Salad with Roasted Butternut Squash and Hazelnuts

Nicoise Salad with Roasted Butternut Squash and Hazelnuts: This delectable salad is a hearty and comforting dinner option. Packed with healthy ingredients like roasted butternut squash, protein-rich tuna, creamy feta, crunchy hazelnuts and a simple vinaigrette, you'll get a full serving of flavor and nutrition in one dish.

Serving: 4 | Preparation Time: 20 minutes | Ready Time: 40 minutes

Ingredients:
- 2 cups cubed butternut squash
- 2 tablespoons olive oil
- Salt and pepper, to taste
- 1 can (6 ounces) tuna, drained
- 1 cup cooked new potatoes, cubed
- 4 cups baby spinach
- 2 cups cherry tomatoes, halved
- 8 pitted kalamata olives
- 1/2 cup crumbled feta
- 1/4 cup roasted hazelnuts
- 4 tablespoons red wine vinaigrette

Instructions:
1. Preheat oven to 425F.
2. In a bowl, toss butternut squash with olive oil and season with salt and pepper. Spread squash onto a baking sheet and roast in the oven for 15 minutes, until squash is tender and lightly browned.
3. Divide baby spinach, cherry tomatoes and olives among four plates. Add cubed potatoes and tuna. Top with crumbled feta and roasted squash.
4. Drizzle with red wine vinaigrette and top with hazelnuts. Serve and enjoy.

Nutrition Information:
Per Serving: Calories: 309; Total Fat: 16g; Cholesterol: 21mg; Sodium: 379mg; Carbohydrates: 24g; Fiber: 4g; Protein: 15g.

82. Nicoise Salad with Cucumber Ribbon Salad

Nicoise Salad with Cucumber Ribbon Salad is a delicious and healthy side dish that features a combination of fresh vegetables and flavors. This salad provides a refreshing and light meal option that requires no cooking and is full of vitamins and minerals.

Serving: 4 | Preparation Time: 10 minutes | Ready Time: 10 minutes

Ingredients:
- 4 tsp Olive Oil
- 2 tsp Red Wine Vinegar
- 2 tbsp Dijon Mustard
- 2 cloves minced Garlic
- 2 Cucumbers, sliced into thin ribbons
- 2 Tomatoes, diced
- 1/2 Green Pepper, diced
- 1/2 cup Kalamata Olives, pitted
- 1/2 cup Corn Kernels
- 2 cups Arugula
- Salt and Pepper, to taste

Instructions:
1. In a large bowl, whisk together the olive oil, red wine vinegar, Dijon mustard, garlic, salt and pepper.
2. Add cucumbers, tomatoes, green peppers, olives, and corn and stir everything together.
3. Add the arugula and mix until the vegetables are evenly distributed.
4. Plate the Nicoise Salad and serve.

Nutrition Information:
Per serving - Calories: 153, Fat: 11 g, Saturated Fat: 2 g, Protein: 3 g, Cholesterol: 0 mg, Sodium: 176 mg, Carbohydrates: 11 g, Fiber: 2 g, Sugar: 5 g

83. Nicoise Salad with Roasted Brussels Sprouts

Nicoise Salad with Roasted Brussels Sprouts is a delicious and nutritious dish. It combines the natural sweetness of roasted Brussels sprouts with tuna, egg and olives for a light and healthy meal.

Serving: 4 | Preparation Time: 10 minutes | Ready Time: 25 minutes

Ingredients:
• 1/2 pound Brussels sprouts, trimmed and halved
• 1/4 cup extra-virgin olive oil, plus more for drizzling
• 2 tablespoons freshly squeezed lemon juice
• 2 tablespoons chopped, fresh parsley
• 4 cups mixed greens
• 1 (7-ounce) can tuna, drained
• 4 hard-boiled eggs, peeled and quartered
• 1/2 cup black olives
• Salt and freshly ground black pepper, to taste

Instructions:
1. Preheat the oven to 375F.
2. Line a baking sheet with parchment paper.
3. Place the Brussels sprouts on the baking sheet and drizzle with olive oil to coat.
4. Roast the Brussels sprouts in the preheated oven for 25 minutes, stirring occasionally, until tender and lightly browned.
5. As the Brussels sprouts roast, whisk together the lemon juice, olive oil and parsley in a large bowl.
6. Add the mixed greens, tuna, eggs and olives, and toss to combine.
7. Add the roasted Brussels sprouts to the bowl and gently toss to combine.
8. Season with salt and pepper, to taste.
9. Serve with a drizzle of olive oil, if desired.

84. Nicoise Salad with Creamy Horseradish Dressing

Nicoise Salad with Creamy Horseradish Dressing is a flavorful and hearty salad for lunch or dinner. Prepared with healthy and fresh ingredients, this salad will have your taste buds asking for more.

Serves 4. | Preparation Time: 10 minutes. | Ready Time: 10 minutes.

Ingredients:
- 4 cups mixed baby greens
- 2 cups cherry tomatoes, halved
- 2 cups small white potatoes, boiled and chopped
- 1/2 cup canned tuna or anchovies
- 1/2 cup green beans, blanched
- 1/2 cup black olives
- 4 hard-boiled eggs, chopped
- 2 tablespoons freshly grated horseradish
- 1/4 cup mayonnaise
- 2 tablespoons lemon juice

Instructions:
1. In a large bowl, combine the baby greens, tomatoes, potatoes, tuna or anchovies, green beans, olives, and eggs.
2. In a medium bowl, whisk together the horseradish, mayonnaise, and lemon juice until combined.
3. Drizzle the dressing over the salad, and toss until the salad is evenly coated with the dressing.
4. Serve the salad immediately while still warm.

Nutrition Information:
Serving size: 2 cups
Calories: 240
Fat: 12g

Carbohydrates: 24g
Protein: 15g

85. Nicoise Salad with Seared Tuna Steak

Nicoise Salad with Seared Tuna Steak is a French-inspired healthy meal, filled with a flavorful combination of tuna, tomatoes, onions, olives, potatoes and eggs, served with a light dressing. Perfect for lunch or dinner, this colorful dish is sure to please everyone.

Serving: 4 | Preparation Time: 15 minutes | Ready Time: 15 minutes

Ingredients:
- 4 tuna steaks
- 2 tablespoons olive oil
- Salt and pepper
- 2 large tomatoes, cut into wedges
- 1/2 cup red onion, thinly sliced
- 1/2 cup pitted black olives
- 1 cup cooked small potatoes (cut into bite-sized pieces)
- 2 hard boiled eggs, peeled and quartered
- 3 tablespoons vinaigrette

Instructions:
1. Heat a large skillet over medium-high heat. Add the olive oil and let it heat up.
2. Rub each of the tuna steaks with the desired amount of salt and pepper.
3. Place the tuna steaks in the hot skillet and let them sear for about 3 minutes on each side.
4. Remove the tuna from the heat and let it cool.
5. In a bowl, add the tomatoes, red onion, black olives, potatoes and eggs.
6. Thinly slice the tuna and place it on top.
7. Drizzle the vinaigrette over the salad.
8. Serve.

Nutrition Information:
Calories: 283
Fat: 14 g
Carbohydrates: 12 g
Protein: 26 g
Saturated Fat: 2.5 g
Sodium: 268 mg
Fiber: 2.5 g

86. Nicoise Salad with Red Quinoa

Nicoise Salad with Red Quinoa is a deliciously light and healthy salad made up of fresh vegetables and quinoa, perfect for a summer day. The protein-rich red quinoa makes a great filling meal, while the colorful vegetables give it a great pop of flavor.

Serving: 4 | Preparation Time: 15 minutes | Ready Time: 15 minutes

Ingredients:
- 2 cups red quinoa
- 2 tomatoes, sliced
- 1 cup artichoke hearts
- 1 cup green beans, trimmed
- 1/4 cup olives
- 1/4 cup feta cheese, crumbled
- 1/4 cup Fresh basil, chopped
- 2 tablespoons olive oil
- 2 tablespoons red wine vinegar
- Salt and pepper, to taste

Instructions:
1. Cook the red quinoa according to package instructions.
2. Once the quinoa is cooked, cool it down and transfer it to a large bowl.
3. Add the tomatoes, artichoke hearts, green beans, olives, feta cheese, and basil to the bowl and mix everything together.
4. In a small bowl, whisk together the olive oil, red wine vinegar, salt, and pepper and pour it over the quinoa mixture.

5. Gently stir everything together until the dressing is evenly distributed.

Nutrition Information (per serving):
Calories: 366, Total Fat: 17g, Saturated Fat: 4g, Trans Fat: 0g,
Cholesterol: 12mg, Sodium: 380mg, Carbohydrates: 39g, Fiber: 6g, Sugar:
4g, Protein: 10g.

87. Nicoise Salad with Fried Capers

Nicoise Salad with Fried Capers is a fresh and flavorful salad that features fresh vegetables and proteins like tuna and hard-boiled eggs. The crisp and tangy fried capers serve to brighten up the salad, making this a delicious and satisfying meal.

Serving: 4 | Preparation Time: 15 minutes | Ready Time: 15 minutes

Ingredients:
- 2 cans wild tuna, drained
- 2 hard-boiled eggs, chopped into small pieces
- 2 cups green simply lettuce, torn into bite-sized pieces
- 2 tomatoes, diced
- 1 red onion, thinly sliced
- 1/2 cup pitted Kalamata olives
- 1/4 cup capers, fried
- 1/4 cup extra-virgin olive oil
- 2 tablespoons white wine vinegar
- Salt and pepper, to taste

Instructions:
1. In a large bowl, combine the tuna, eggs, lettuce, tomatoes, red onions, and olives.
2. In a medium bowl, whisk together the extra-virgin olive oil, white wine vinegar, salt, and pepper.
3. Drizzle the dressing over the salad and toss to combine.
4. Sprinkle the fried capers over the salad and serve.

Nutrition Information:
Calories: 324, Total Fat: 22.5 g, Cholesterol: 105 mg, Total
Carbohydrates: 8.5 g, Fiber: 2.4 g, Protein: 20.5 g

88. Nicoise Salad with Pickled Mustard Seed Dressing

Nicoise Salad with Pickled Mustard Seed Dressing is a vibrant and
flavorful medley of flavors and textures. This simple, yet satisfying lunch
option makes use of fresh, ripe veggies, salty tuna, and a sharp, slightly
sweet mustard seed dressing.

Serving: 4 | Preparation Time: 10 minutes | Ready Time: 20 minutes

Ingredients:
For the Salad:
• 1 head Romaine lettuce, washed and chopped
• 2 cans (7.5-ounce) tuna packed in oil, drained
• 1 large red bell pepper, seeds removed, diced
• 2 small tomatoes, quartered
• 1 cup cooked green beans
• 1/2 cup pitted black olives
• 2 hard-boiled eggs, quartered
For the Dressing:
• 1/4 cup red wine vinegar
• 1/4 cup dijon mustard
• 1 tablespoon pickled mustard seeds
• 1 teaspoon honey
• 1/2 cup extra virgin olive oil
• Salt and pepper to taste

Instructions:
1. To prepare the salad, combine the romaine lettuce, tuna, red pepper,
tomatoes, green beans, olives and eggs in a large bowl and toss gently to
combine.
2. To prepare the dressing, whisk together the red wine vinegar, dijon
mustard, pickled mustard seeds, honey, olive oil, salt and pepper in a
small bowl until fully combined.

3. Drizzle the dressing over the salad and toss to combine. Serve immediately.

Nutrition Information:
Serving size: 1/4 of recipe
Calories: 296
Total Fat: 17g
Saturated Fat: 3g
Cholesterol: 89mg
Sodium: 297mg

Carbohydrate: 14g
Fiber: 3g
Sugar: 7g
Protein: 23g

89. Nicoise Salad with Toasted Sesame Seeds

Nicoise Salad with Toasted Sesame Seeds is a delicious and nutritious salad full of fresh, flavorful ingredients. This flavorful dish includes tuna, hard-boiled eggs, olives, tomatoes, and a simple dressing of red wine vinegar, olive oil, and toasted sesame seeds.

Serving: 4-6 | Preparation Time: 15 minutes

Ingredients:
- 4-6 oz. canned tuna, drained
- 2 hard-boiled eggs, cut into slices
- 1/4 cup black olives
- 2 medium tomatoes, sliced
- 2 tablespoons red wine vinegar
- 1 tablespoon extra-virgin olive oil
- 1 tablespoon toasted sesame seeds

Instructions:
1. In a large bowl, combine the canned tuna, hard-boiled eggs, olives, and tomatoes.

2. In a separate bowl, whisk together the red wine vinegar, olive oil, and toasted sesame seeds to make the dressing.
3. Pour the dressing over the salad, tossing to combine.

Nutrition Information:
Calories 143 kcal, Protein 12.9 g, Total Carbohydrate 4.1 g, Total Fat 8.7 g, Saturated Fat 1.2 g, Sodium 380 mg, Potassium 211 mg.

90. Nicoise Salad with Smoked Salmon

Nicoise Salad with Smoked Salmon is a unique, delightful French salad that pairs fresh lettuce with smoked salmon, Nicoise olives, hard boiled eggs, and a delicious vinaigrette dressing. It is both flavorful and healthy, and makes for a perfect side dish or main course.

Serving: 4 | Preparation Time: 10 minutes | Ready Time: 10 minutes

Ingredients:
- 2 Large heads of Lettuce, washed and chopped
- 2 Smoked Salmon Filets
- 2 Hard Boiled Eggs, chopped
- 1/2 cup Nicoise Olives, pitted
- 2 tablespoons Olive Oil
- 2 tablespoons White Wine Vinegar
- 1 tablespoon Dijon Mustard
- Salt and Pepper, to taste

Instructions:
1. In a large bowl, combine the chopped lettuce, smoked salmon, hard boiled eggs, and Nicoise olives.
2. In a small bowl, whisk together the olive oil, white wine vinegar, dijon mustard, salt, and pepper. Pour over the salad and mix everything together to combine.
3. Serve immediately.

Nutrition Information:
Calories: 350, Fat: 23 g, Protein: 21 g, Cholesterol: 130 mg, Sodium: 550 mg, Carbohydrates: 18 g, Fiber: 5 g.

91. Nicoise Salad with Roasted Walnuts

This Nicoise Salad with Roasted Walnuts is a light, refreshing and bursting with flavor. Perfect for a summer lunch or dinner, it's also great for special occasions or as a side dish.

Serving: Makes 4 servings | Preparation Time: 20 minutes | Ready Time: 20 minutes

Ingredients:

- 2 heads of butter lettuce, washed, dried and torn into bite-sized pieces
- 6 cups mixed green vegetables, such as sugar snap peas, thin asparagus, string beans
- 1 large cucumber, peeled and cut into bite-sized pieces
- 1 large red bell pepper, seeded, cored and chopped
- 2 tomatoes, seeded and chopped
- 1/4 cup olive oil
- 2 tablespoons Dijon mustard
- 4 cloves garlic, minced
- 1/2 teaspoon fresh ground pepper
- 1/4 teaspoon kosher salt
- 1 teaspoon dried oregano
- 1 cup shelled walnuts

Instructions:

1. Preheat the oven to 350 degrees F.
2. Spread the walnuts on a baking sheet, and roast in the preheated oven for 8 minutes, stirring once, until lightly toasted. Set aside.
3. In a medium bowl, whisk together the olive oil, mustard, garlic, pepper, salt, and oregano until well blended.
4. In a large bowl, combine the lettuce, green vegetables, cucumber, bell pepper, and tomatoes.
5. Pour the dressing over the salad and toss to coat.
6. Divide the salad among 4 plates, and top each with a quarter of the roasted walnuts.

Nutrition Information (per serving):
Calories: 178
Fat: 14.7 g
Saturated Fat: 1.8 g
Carbohydrates: 10.5 g
Fiber: 4.4 g
Protein: 4.4 g

92. Nicoise Salad with Pickled Asparagus

Nicoise Salad with Pickled Asparagus is a Mediterranean-style salad with bright flavors, crunchy vegetables and pickled asparagus. It is easy to make and offers a great way to enjoy some fresh produce.

Serving: 8 | Preparation Time: 15 minutes | Ready Time: 25 minutes

Ingredients:
- 1 pound asparagus, trimmed
- 2 tablespoons olive oil
- 2 cloves garlic, minced
- 2 tablespoons balsamic vinegar
- 1 tablespoon pickling spice
- Juice of 1 lemon
- 1 teaspoon sugar
- 2 cups cherry tomatoes, quartered
- 2 cups lettuce, chopped
- 1/2 cup black olives, pitted
- 1/4 cup feta cheese, crumbled
- 2 tablespoons fresh basil, chopped

Instructions:
1. Preheat oven to 375F.
2. Place asparagus on a baking sheet, drizzle with olive oil and garlic, and roast for 8 minutes.
3. In a small saucepan, whisk together balsamic vinegar, pickling spice, sugar, lemon juice and 2 tablespoons of water. Bring to a boil, reduce heat and simmer until reduced by half.

4. Place asparagus in a bowl, pour over the balsamic reduction and let cool.

5. In a large bowl, combine tomatoes, lettuce, olives, feta cheese and basil.

6. Add the cooled asparagus and toss to combine.

7. Serve chilled.

Nutrition Information: (per serving)
Calories: 92 kcal; Fat: 5.6 g; Cholesterol: 9 mg; Sodium: 115mg; Carbohydrates: 8.5g; Protein: 4.0g; Fiber: 2.5g.

93. Nicoise Salad with Caviar

Nicoise Salad with Caviar is a French inspired dish, the perfect combination of flavors that's both elegant and flavorful. It's a great appetizer or light meal to impress your guests.

Serving: 4-6 | Preparation Time: 15 minutes | Ready Time: 15 minutes

Ingredients:
-4-5 anchovy fillets
-1 head of Romaine lettuce, chopped
-1 cup of steamed and cooled green beans
-1/4 cup of diced red onion
-1/2 cup of sliced cherry tomatoes
-1/4 cup of pitted and sliced black olives
-1/4 cup of cooked miniature potatoes
-2 tablespoons of extra-virgin olive oil
-2 tablespoons of white balsamic vinegar
-1 tablespoon of Dijon mustard
-1 teaspoon of minced garlic
-4-6 ounces of caviar
-salt and pepper to taste

Instructions:
1. Start by boiling the potatoes until they're soft. Let cool.
2. In a bowl whisk together olive oil, balsamic vinegar, garlic, and mustard and season with salt and pepper.

3. In a large bowl combine Romaine lettuce, eggs, green beans, red onion, cherry tomatoes, and olives.
4. Gently fold in the cooled potatoes and pour over the dressing.
5. Top with anchovy fillets and caviar.

Nutrition Information:
Calories: 191 kcal/serving,
Carbohydrates: 12.5 g/serving,
Protein: 8.5 g/serving,
Cholesterol: 32 mg/serving,
Total Fat: 11 g/serving,
Sodium: 465 mg/serving.

94. Nicoise Salad with Grilled Eggplant

Nicoise Salad with Grilled Eggplant is a fresh, flavorful and healthy dish that is perfect for a light lunch or dinner. This plant-based salad combines grilled eggplant, whole grain faro, cherry tomatoes, roasted peppers and olives to create a delicious and colorful meal.

Serving: 4 | Preparation Time: 15 minutes | Ready Time: 15 minutes

Ingredients:
- 2 Eggplants, halves lengthwise
- 1/2 cup Faro, cooked
- 1/2 cup Cherry Tomatoes, halved
- 1/4 cup Roasted Red Peppers, sliced
- 1/4 cup Kalamata Olives
- 2 tablespoons Parsley, chopped
- 2 tablespoons Olive Oil
- 1 teaspoon Balsamic Vinegar
- 2 teaspoons Thyme
- Salt and Pepper, to taste

Instructions:
1. Preheat your grill on high and brush each eggplant half with olive oil, salt and pepper.

2. Place eggplant halves onto the grill and cook for 7 minutes on each side, or until eggplant is golden brown.
3. Once eggplant is cooked through, remove from the grill and let cool for a few minutes.
4. In a large bowl, combine faro, cherry tomatoes, roasted red peppers and olives.
5. Slice cooked eggplant into thin strips and add to the bowl.
6. Add parsley, olive oil, balsamic vinegar, thyme and additional salt and pepper to the bowl and mix together.
7. Serve Nicoise Salad with Grilled Eggplant.

Nutrition Information:
100 calories per serving; 4g fat, 16g carbohydrates, and 4g protein.

95. Nicoise Salad with Crispy Shallots and Chives

Nicoise Salad with Crispy Shallots and Chives is a flavorful and nutritious mix of fresh greens, salty anchovies, boiled eggs, olives, and shallots. The addition of chives in this recipe adds a subtle garlic-onion flavor and crispy texture. This salad is easy to make and goes perfectly with any meal.

Serving: 4-6 | Preparation Time:15 minutes | Ready Time: 15 minutes

Ingredients:
- 2 tablespoons olive oil
- 2 shallots, thinly sliced
- 2 tablespoons chives, finely chopped
- 2 heads butter lettuce, torn into bite-size pieces
- 1 pint cherry tomatoes, halved
- 2 cans anchovies, drained
- 2 hard boiled eggs, chopped
- 1/4 cup kalamata olives, pitted and halved

Instructions:
1. Heat the olive oil in a large nonstick skillet over medium-high heat.
2. Add the shallots and chives and cook until they are lightly browned and crispy, about 5 minutes.

3. Remove the shallots from the pan and set aside on a plate.
4. In a large bowl, combine the lettuce, tomatoes, anchovies, eggs, and olives.
5. Top with the crispy shallots and chives and drizzle with additional olive oil, if desired.
6. Serve immediately.

Nutrition Information (per serving):
Calories: 150, Fat: 9g, Carbohydrates: 8g, Protein: 6g, Fiber: 3g, Sodium: 450mg.

96. Nicoise Salad with Roasted Carrots

This Nicoise Salad with Roasted Carrots is a delicious and colourful salad perfect for any occasion! It is packed full of flavour, colourful veggies, and the slightly charred taste of roasted carrots. It will be a hit for everyone who loves salads!

Serving: 4-5 | Preparation Time: 10 minutes | Ready Time: 25 minutes

Ingredients:
- 2 bunches of rainbow carrots, trimmed & washed
- 2 tablespoons of olive oil
- 2 tablespoons of honey
- 1 clove of garlic, minced
- 1 head of romaine lettuce, washed and cut into thinner strips
- 1/4 cup capers, rinsed
- 6-8 cherry tomatoes, halved
- 3 anchovy fillets, chopped
- 2 hard-boiled eggs, peeled & sliced
- 1/4 cup black olives
- 2 tablespoons of balsamic vinegar

Instructions:
1. Preheat oven to 375 degrees F.

2. Line a baking sheet with parchment paper, and spread carrots onto the parchment paper. Drizzle carrots with olive oil and honey and season with garlic powder, salt and pepper.
3. Roast carrots for 15-20 minutes, or until golden and slightly charred.
4. In a large bowl, combine romaine lettuce, capers, cherry tomatoes, anchovy fillets, hard-boiled eggs, black olives and roasted carrots.
5. Toss with balsamic vinegar and season with salt and pepper to taste.

Nutrition Information:
Calories: 192, Total Fat: 8 g, Saturated Fat: 2 g, Cholesterol: 99 mg, Sodium: 580 mg, Carbohydrates: 22 g, Fiber: 6 g, Sugar: 11 g, Protein: 8 g

97. Nicoise Salad with Red Wine Vinaigrette

Nicoise Salad with Red Wine Vinaigrette is a hearty and flavorful Mediterranean-inspired salad that is perfect for serving alongside a warm summer meal. It features a combination of fresh vegetables and tuna, all marinated in a tangy red wine vinaigrette. The vinaigrette is prepared quickly and easily with a few simple pantry staples, bringing this salad to life in only 20 minutes.

Serving: 4-6 | Preparation Time: 10 minutes | Ready Time: 20 minutes

Ingredients:
- 4 cups chopped Romaine lettuce
- 1/2 lb. fresh green beans, trimmed
- 1/2 red onion, thinly sliced
- 2 ripe tomatoes, diced
- 15-ounce can tuna, drained
- 2 hard-boiled eggs, sliced
- 10 black olives (optional)
- 2 tablespoons red wine vinegar
- 4 tablespoons extra-virgin olive oil
- 1 teaspoon Dijon mustard
- Salt and pepper, to taste

Instructions:
1. Place lettuce in a large bowl; add green beans, onion, tomatoes, tuna, eggs and olives (optional).
2. In a small bowl, whisk together red wine vinegar, olive oil and Dijon mustard. Season with salt and pepper and whisk until blended.
3. Pour the vinaigrette over the salad and toss gently to combine. Serve immediately.

Nutrition Information:
per serving:
Calories: 336 Fat: 21g Carbohydrates: 11.6g Protein: 24g Fiber: 2.7g
Sodium: 290mg Cholesterol: 125mg

98. Nicoise Salad with Honey Mustard Dressing

Nicoise Salad with Honey Mustard Dressing is a light and flavorful salad. It is the perfect dish for a summer dinner and takes less than twenty minutes to prepare.

Serving: 6 | Preparation Time: 10 minutes | Ready Time: 20 minutes

Ingredients:
- 5 tablespoons honey
- 2 tablespoons Dijon mustard
- 2 tablespoons olive oil
- Juice of 1 lemon
- 2 cups mixed greens
- 1 can (14 ounces) black olives, drained and rinsed
- 1 cup cooked small potatoes, quartered
- 1 tomato, chopped
- 1 can (6 ounces) tuna, drained and flaked
- 2 hard-boiled eggs, quartered

Instructions:
1. In a small bowl, whisk together honey, mustard, olive oil and lemon juice until combined.
2. Divide greens among plates.
3. Top with olives, potatoes, tomatoes, tuna, and eggs.

4. Drizzle with honey mustard dressing.

Nutrition Information:
Calories: 174; Protein: 8.8g; Carbohydrates: 20.4g; Fat: 6.8g; Fiber: 2.4g;
Cholesterol: 66mg; Sodium: 444mg.

99. Nicoise Salad with Orange Slices

Nicoise Salad with Orange Slices is a delicious Mediterranean-style salad
that packs a delightful flavor. This unique salad combines traditional
Nicoise ingredients like canned tuna and boiled eggs with sweet and juicy
orange slices, making it a dish that guests will love.

Serves 6, | Preparation Time: 15 minutes, | Ready Time: 20 minutes.

Ingredients:
- 2 cans of tuna
- 4 boiled eggs, chopped
- 2 oranges, sliced
- 2 cups of Romaine lettuce, chopped
- 1 cup of cherry tomatoes, cut into halves
- 1/4 cup of black olives, pitted
- 1/4 cup of extra-virgin olive oil
- 1 teaspoon of French mustard
- 1 teaspoon of lemon juice
- Salt and pepper, to taste

Instructions:
1. In a large bowl, combine the tuna, boiled eggs, lettuce, cherry
tomatoes, and olives.
2. In a small bowl, whisk together the olive oil, mustard, lemon juice, salt
and pepper.
3. Add the dressing to the tuna mixture, and toss to coat.
4. Divide the salad into 6 individual bowls and top each one with orange
slices.

Nutrition Information (per serving):
Calories: 253 calories
Total Fat: 9.7g
Cholesterol: 68mg
Sodium: 270mg
Carbohydrates: 17.6g
Protein: 25.9g

100. Nicoise Salad with Radishes and Asparagus

Nicoise Salad with Radishes and Asparagus is a light and flavorful dish perfect for a summertime lunch or dinner. The combination of crunchy asparagus, tangy radishes and flavorful vinaigrette creates a dish that's as satisfying as it is healthy.

Servings: 4 | Preparation Time: 20 minutes | Ready Time: 20 minutes

Ingredients:
- 1 pound asparagus
- 4 radishes, thinly sliced
- 1 tablespoon Dijon mustard
- 2 tablespoons red wine vinegar
- 4 tablespoons olive oil
- 2 tablespoons capers
- 6 anchovy filets
- 4 cups lettuce
- 2 hardboiled eggs, coarsely chopped
- Salt and pepper, to taste

Instructions:
1. Trim the bottom of the asparagus and cut into 1-inch pieces. Bring a small pot of salted water to a boil, add the asparagus and blanch for 1 minute. Drain and run the asparagus under cold water to stop it from cooking.
2. In a medium bowl, whisk together the mustard, red wine vinegar, olive oil, capers and anchovy filets.

3. Put the lettuce on a serving plate and top with the asparagus and radishes. Drizzle with the vinaigrette and sprinkle with the chopped hard-boiled eggs.
4. Season with salt and pepper and serve.

Nutrition Information:
Per Serving: 163 calories, 12 grams fat, 5.5 grams carbs, 7.5 grams protein.

101. Nicoise Salad with Roasted Prosciutto and Pine Nuts

Nicoise Salad with Roasted Prosciutto and Pine Nuts is a hearty and flavorful European inspired salad. It is the perfect combination of fresh garden vegetables, juicy tomatoes, salty prosciutto, and nutty pine nuts, making it a satisfying and nutritious dish.

Serving: 4-6 | Preparation Time: 15 minutes | Ready Time: 20 minutes

Ingredients:
- 2 tablespoons olive oil
- 6 slices of prosciutto
- 1/4 cup pine nuts
- 1 small head of Romaine lettuce, chopped
- 1/2 small cucumber, sliced
- 1 small red onion, sliced
- 1/2 cup cherry tomatoes, halved
- 2 tablespoons balsamic vinegar
- Fresh cracked pepper

Instructions:
1. Preheat the oven to 350F. Line a baking sheet with foil and spray with nonstick cooking spray.
2. Toss the prosciutto slices in the olive oil and spread them onto the baking sheet. Bake for 10 minutes, or until crispy. Remove from the oven and let cool.
3. Place pine nuts in a small skillet over medium heat. Toast for 2-3 minutes, or until lightly golden and fragrant.

4. In a large bowl, combine the lettuce, cucumber, red onion, cherry tomatoes, and balsamic vinegar and toss to coat.

5. Top with the roasted prosciutto and toasted pine nuts and season with fresh cracked pepper.

Nutrition Information:

Calories: 180
Fat: 13g
Carbohydrates: 8g
Protein: 10g

CONCLUSION `

The Ultimate Nicoise Salad Cookbook provides 101 delicious recipes for every occasion. From simple and straightforward starters and sides, to complex and hearty mains and meals, this cookbook allows cooks of every ability and lifestyle to enjoy the flavors of the iconic Nicoise salad. Recipes range from familiar interpretations of the classic original to more modern, innovative creations; each one bringing out all the salty, briney, and nourishing flavors of the traditional mediterranean-style dish.

No matter the occasion, the recipes in The Ultimate Nicoise Salad Cookbook can provide a creative and tasty dish for home cooks of all abilities. In addition to traditional style Nicoise salads packed full of olives, anchovies, and other tangy ingredients, these recipes also showcase inventive takes on the classic salad – updated for modern times, or offering vegan- or vegetarian-friendly options. This cookbook also features numerous salads utilizing Whole30-friendly and gluten-free ingredients, allowing all kinds of diets and lifestyles to enjoy healthy, flavorful options.

The recipes in The Ultimate Nicoise Salad Cookbook are perfect for light summertime meals, impressing guests at a dinner party, or prepping powerhouse lunches. Each recipe is designed to be easy-to-follow and stress-free, with straightforward instructions that are easy to master and adapt. With these 101 eclectic and delicious recipes, home cooks will be able to celebrate the iconic Nicoise salad successfully and confidently, no matter the occasion.

Printed in Great Britain
by Amazon

34317781R00059